Forever Rescued

How Jesus Set Me Free

Carol Drinkwater Gauthier

ISBN 978-1-0980-7382-4 (paperback)
ISBN 978-1-0980-7383-1 (digital)

Christian Faith Publishing, Inc.
832 Park Avenue
Meadville, PA 16335
www.christianfaithpublishing.com

Some of the names that are in this book have been changed to protect their identity.

Printed in the United States of America

I dedicate this book to my husband, my wonderful family, and my great friends and prayer partners. I cannot forget to thank my tech support and faithful friend Jerry who was there for me whenever I called on him; day or night he was always available. I could not have completed this journey without the help and support from all of you. I am forever grateful for your patience, prayers, and love. Thank you!

My legacy to you is my life in Jesus Christ; and may you always know how much I love you! Know, too, how much I love my Father God, His Son Jesus Christ, and His Holy Spirit. Know that Jesus Christ is the name that is above all names! I will let every second of my life point only to Jesus Christ because His name is the only name that will last forever. My hope is that I lived the truth to the ones I love and that my life was lived for Him and through Him. Yes, I know that I have made a lot of mistakes, and I have made some bad choices, but praise to God who has forgiven me and washed me clean to make me a new creation in Him. My prayer is that in your journey of life, may you know the power of His grace and love.

Grace is one of God's most amazing gifts to us. It provides us with everything we need to live in perfect freedom—pardoned from our sins, healing for our hearts, the companionship of God's indwelling Holy Spirit, and access to freely cultivate our relationship with Him. We work, worship, and enjoy life surrounded by His unconditional love. His grace upholds us, fills us, and sustains us. Since we are forgiven people, the Lord responds to us not as enemies but as His dearly beloved children. He hears our prayers, speaks to us, and acts on our behalf. The knowledge that we live under the covering of God's grace gives us…*security* about our position. No one can snatch us out of His hand see (John 10:28). We have been given *boldness* to live for Christ. There is nothing anyone can do or say that can shake our confidence in who the Lord is and how much He loves us. He gives us *peace* for today because we can fully trust in His power and His sovereignty. The Lord is carrying out His perfect will—and we can be sure that nothing is able to thwart His plans when we cooperate with Him. He gives us *hope* for the future because this life is just the beginning. One day we'll see Jesus face-to-face and be perfected as the individuals He created us to be, and we will live with Him in our true home forever. The Lord is committed to transforming each of us according to His special plan for our lives. Even His correction is an expression of His loving favor. When we falter or fail, we can rest assured that His *amazing grace* hems us in and always offers us redemption. Hallelujah, and praise God forever!

A Word from God...

My child, never forget the things I have taught you. Store my commands in your heart. If you do this, you will live many years, and your life will be satisfying. Never let loyalty and kindness leave you! Tie them around your neck as reminders. Write them deep within your heart. Then you will find favor with both God and people, and you will earn a good reputation. Trust in the LORD with all your heart; do not depend on your own understanding. Seek his will in all you do, and he will show you which path to take. (Proverbs 3:1–10)

I will rescue those who love me and I will protect those who trust in my Name. (Psalm 91:14)

How beautiful on the mountains are the feet of the messenger who brings good news, the good news of peace and salvation, the news that the God of Israel reigns! (Isaiah 52:7)

Introduction

It is 3:00 a.m., and the Lord has awakened me again to write my story. I commit this book to the Lord who has called me *the pen of a skillful writer*.

> My heart is stirred by a noble theme as
> I recite my verses for the King; my tongue is
> the pen of a skillful writer. (Psalm 45:1)

I have learned that all honor and glory must go to our God and Savior Who created us, Who sanctifies us, and Who sustains us. He has specific tasks for us in order to further His kingdom and to bring all glory, honor and praise to Him alone. His powerful hand is at work for each of us, and in my case, He said that I am the pen of a skillful writer. Therefore, He wants to use my life so I can see His powerful hand at work in and through me, and I will praise Him throughout my life. That is why I am writing this book. Because through it all, I have learned to trust in Him and to take Him at His Word, and He has never disappointed me, left me, or forsaken me.

> I give them eternal life, and they will
> never perish. No one can snatch them away
> from me, for my Father has given them
> to me, and he is more powerful than any-
> one else. No one can snatch them from the
> Father's hand. (John 10:28–29)

Now, Lord, it is fitting that *You* give me the words to share my story.

This is a story of deliverance from captivity and the *Deliverer* Who so lovingly reached down to set me free. It becomes the story of healing—healing from the many consequences of being a captive. It will also be the story of the many ways in which God, my *Deliverer,* continues to work miraculously within the lives of captives and the freed alike.

Parts of this story will not be easy to tell, but the message is one of hope, one of love and grace, and one of our loving heavenly Father Who turns ALL things around for good for those Who love Him.

> And I am convinced that nothing can ever separate us from God's love. Neither death nor life, neither angels nor demons, neither our fears for today nor our worries about tomorrow—not even the powers of hell can separate us from God's love. No power in the sky above or in the earth below—indeed, nothing in all creation will ever be able to separate us from the love of God that is revealed in Christ Jesus our Lord. (Romans 8:38–39)

Beginning a story is always the hardest part of telling a story. This one is no different. I have tried to go back to the "beginning" and chronicle life's events to the present...in other words, tell a *long* story. However, I'd like to begin at the point wherein I realized that I was living a life I was not designed to live—a life being lived in captivity. When I think back on that time, what stands out most are the remembrances of desperately looking for a "way out." A way out of *what,* I wasn't sure; I just knew I needed a way out. My life felt as though it had become a stormy mix of feelings and actions resulting from a loveless, abusive childhood with no protection. A heavy cloud of depression had so settled over me that I couldn't find a *light* in the darkness. It is a story of my *rescue* by the *Deliverer* Who set me free and the miracles He performed on my journey to freedom. You may come to understand why a child would feel unloved and rejected when you learned that your parents tried to abort you on three occasions but were unsuccessful. It was because I was born with a spirit of rejection, and I didn't know how to escape. I often wondered if the trials and tribulations one might have encountered before birth were necessary in order to be *rescued* by a loving and holy God.

> You made all the delicate, inner parts of my body and knit me together in my mother's womb. Thank you for making me so wonderfully complex! Your workmanship is marvelous—how well I know it. You watched me as I was being formed in utter seclusion, as I was woven together in the darkness of the womb. You saw me before I was born. Every day of my life was recorded in your book. Every moment was laid out before a single day had passed. (Psalm 139:15–16)

Lord, this book will explain why my mother was *rescued* from that tragic fire in 1942 and why my parents were not able to abort me after trying three times with no success. It is because You are Almighty God and You chose to *rescue* me, but first You had to *rescue* my mother in order to *rescue* me.

You have since given me Your Holy Bible to read and study because it is the truth, and because now that I belong to You, I no longer need to live a life of feelings, lies, and deceit. You had a divine purpose and plan for my life! You said now I am free to live, move, and have my being in YOU. Father, let Your perfect will be done in and through me. I thank You, Father, for *RESCUING* me, for saving my soul, and for making me whole. Thank You, Lord, for giving to me Thy great salvation which is so rich and so free.

Prologue

This is a story of my family—a hardworking Italian American family that lived in East Boston, Massachusetts. I am the narrator of this story.

I was born in an elevator in Winthrop, Massachusetts, at five o'clock in the morning of June 26, 1946. I am the second child, born eleven months after my sister. I guess you can call me an Irish twin. I lived what might be called a secret life—because in those days, you did not dare tell the truth; therefore, you were entrapped in fear.

Sometimes it is the message that parents send to their children and how that child receives it. Parents are communicators. Everything they do and say will mold their children for life; it will illustrate their priorities, their beliefs, and even their sins. Your entire childhood can be ruined depending on how the child receives the positive or the negative messages. Troubled and angry parents can do great harm to their children, who can be wounded for life. I have learned that a home without God and His wisdom can be dreadful...and a home with God's presence can be the greatest blessing of all. Praise to God Who can turn all things around for the good when you call on Him for help!

> We can rejoice, when we run into problems
> and trials, for we know that they help us develop
> endurance. And endurance develops strength of
> character, and character strengthens our confi-
> dent hope of salvation. (Romans 5:3–4)

But then you may ask, "Why does God allow these trials and tribulations?" At the time that we are suffering, we may not know God is walking through them with us—at least I didn't—especially because we do not know God and His ways. We are feeling the pain, so how can we know He is suffering with us. As you will read in this book, God uses these experiences so that we will finally call upon Him for help. He will open our eyes to our sins that we have tolerated in our life so that we turn to Him and repent. All humanity was born in sin, and that is why God sent His only begotten Son, Jesus Christ, to set the captives free. He must also discipline us to produce the fruits of His righteousness and purify us so He can transform us into His image and likeness. Plus, He wants our suffering to produce His power in us so we will call out to Him for help and, like I said, repent of our sins so that we can accept Jesus Christ into our hearts and be set free. Once we accept Jesus into our hearts, He can then develop character and maturity in us. He could even be testing us to see if we will produce faith, endurance, and devotion to Him. Then we can rejoice when we run into problems, trials, and tribulations. For we know that they help to develop endurance. Endurance develops strength of character. Character strengthens our confident hope of salvation. So we must trust that Father God knows best and He truly has a plan for our lives! I thank God that, eventually, I did believe, repent, and turn my life over to Jesus Christ and to be saved or born again!

> He will sift us like a refiner of silver,
> burning away the dross. He will purify them
> refining them like gold and silver, so that they
> may once again offer acceptable sacrifices to
> the LORD. (Malachi 3:3)

Our Father God, who seeks to perfect His saints in holiness, knows the value of the refiner's fire. It is with the most precious metals that the assayer takes the most pains, and subjects them to the hot fire, because such fires melt the metal, and only the molten mass releases its alloy or takes perfectly its new form in the mold. The old refiner never leaves his credible, but sits down by it, lest there should be one excessive degree of heat to mar the metal. But as soon as he skims from the surface the last of the dross, and sees his own face reflected, he puts out the fire. (Arthur T. Pierson)

However, you will read that I did live the second half of my life healed and at peace with my God without feeling much inclination to write my story. Until God woke me up on several occasions over the years and told me to write this book to glorify Him. It's the story of the *rescue* of one soul of an ordinary girl who had all the life beaten out of her until she was so lost and hurt that only God could *rescue* her from despair and suicide.

I went through my childhood with actually no childhood at all. I became naked and raw, hopeless and heartless, and full of despair and depression. Sometimes that pain grew worse as the years went on. The longer you bury it, the harder is it to face it and call upon God for help. I was sure that I could find relief, safety, and love in perhaps the next relationship, the next habit, or even the next life…if I only tried hard enough to bury the pain. Suicide became an answer so many times in my life until I found the "*Light*"—Jesus Christ Himself—who came to *rescue* me, redeem me, sanctify me, and give me everlasting life.

Chapter 1

East Boston

My parents and grandparents were all born in Italy. My mother's family settled in East Boston, Massachusetts, and my dad's family settled in New York, then moved to Revere, Everett, and finally Malden, Massachusetts. They all were laborers who worked hard to make a living. My dad drove a truck in Boston for the MBTA, and my mother was a seamstress in East Boston. My mother worked in the basement of her mother's house where they stitched for a clothing company in downtown Boston. They did piecework, and their work was delivered to them on a biweekly basis. They all lived in three-floor tenement buildings in East Boston, and I can remember life being fun with all our Italian relatives and friends. But I remember too that it was a hard life for them as they always struggled to make ends meet.

My father's family moved to Revere, Everett, and then eventually settled in Malden, Massachusetts. I was told that my grandfather was hard on his sons, and they had a rough life enduring anger and physical abuse. My father was an identical twin, and he had two sisters that were also twins. There were three sisters and three brothers, seven kids in all. My grandfather made wine and anisette in his basement and had a small candy store, where he made ribbon candy as well. If we were getting sick or had the chills on a cold winter's day, we were given a shot of anisette, and that always made us feel better. Wine was freely offered at mealtimes, and it always complemented our Italian dinners. My papa and some of his sons were meat cutters in Everett, Massachusetts. Most of my father's family lived in the Malden area, and I enjoyed them all very much. Papa was pretty strong and mean, my dad would tell me, but I didn't get to know him too well as he passed away at an early age of pancreatic cancer. My grandmother, whom we called Nana, was very quiet and meek, and because she lived alone, my dad picked her up for dinner on Sundays after Papa died. My father's two twin sisters lived in the same two-family house with Nana except when one of the twins got married. She bought the house next-door to Nana so they all remained close.

My mother had a sister and three brothers who all lived in East Boston as well. They owned a restaurant and a meat market where some of them were employed. My mother's dad suffered a heart attack when she was a child, and that was when her life changed. She was the second-oldest child, so she had to care for the health and welfare of her family so that her mother could work and support the family. She could recall living a hard life, and she was very close to her father and suffered greatly when he died. She had a younger brother, who had a serious heart condition, so she also had the responsibility of caring for him as well. I was especially fond of my uncles Tony and Joe because they were always there to love and encourage me. My mom said that my grandmother was difficult to live with in those days, carrying all the burdens of raising a family alone. My mother also worked as a stitcher in the basement to help make ends meet.

When my mom was about twenty-two years old, I can remember her telling me the story when she and her friends sneaked out of the house to go dancing which was the dance that almost ended her life. They were at the Cocoanut Grove Restaurant and Club in Boston when it caught on fire, and many lives were lost, including her male friend Fred. But she and her other friends escaped, leaving only scars of fear, fright, and nightmares. She received much punishment from her mother for that mishap. But since she came out alive, she was always thankful to God for *rescuing* her. Here is that story…

My maternal great-grandparents
Rosa & Alexender Tavella

Grandpa and Grandma (my maternal grandparents)
Joseph and Rosina Tavella

my paternal Grandparents
Ralph & Carmella Bevilacqua

Mom and her
sister rescued
from fire

Mom's two brothers
Joe and Tony

History of the Tragedy in Boston

Saturday, November 28, 1942, at the US Navy Yard in Boston, Massachusetts, had been, for the most part, a relatively uneventful day.

According to the duty log, nineteen ships were berthed at the yard or at nearby auxiliary piers along Boston Harbor. Duty officers performing periodic patrols took note of the vessels that navigated in and out of the yard and the South Boston Naval Annex throughout the calm yet freezing-cold day. Indeed, such activity was common for this strategic shipbuilding facility, which produced and repaired numerous vessels for use during World War II.

However, before Saturday had elapsed, the sailors and Marines of the yard would heed a call for aid that was anything but routine.

Boston newspapers greeted their readers with the day's updates of the war in Europe and the Pacific, which, nearly a year after the attack on Pearl Harbor, had become and would continue to be regular practice throughout the war. In late 1942, Bostonians were reading of the Allies' months-long struggle against the Imperial Japanese forces at Guadalcanal and the Soviet Red Army's counteroffensive against the German Sixth Army at Stalingrad.

Local college football fans diverted their attention to Fenway Park for the annual late season Jesuit school rivalry game, in which the Holy Cross Crusaders achieved a stunning 55–12 upset victory, over the top-ranked Boston College Eagles, denying BC an undefeated season and an invitation to the Sugar Bowl.

Despite the outcome of the game, it was Thanksgiving weekend, and many servicemen throughout the First Naval District were looking forward to enjoying leave away from their duties.

For many officers and enlisted men with free time, it was an opportunity for an evening of dinner, drinks, and dancing with their dates. And there were few more desirable places to do just that in Boston than at the famous Cocoanut Grove night club.

For nearly a decade following the end of Prohibition, "The Grove"—located in the Bay Village neighborhood of Boston—was one of the most popular social scenes in the city. Sporting a South Seas-style ambiance, the club treated patrons to food, hospitality, and entertainment, as well as the occasional appearance of music artists or movie stars gracing the dinner-goers with their presence.[*]

On this Saturday night, more than one thousand patrons packed the main dining room and cocktail lounges at the Cocoanut Grove. Despite the cancellation of a Boston College victory celebration after the football team's defeat that afternoon, the club had no difficulty in filling the establishment, especially with a floor show about to begin.

Then suddenly, at approximately 10:15 p.m., a small fire broke out in the club's basement, Melody Lounge. Eyewitnesses recounted that they had first spotted the fire in a decorative palm tree in the lounge, working its way up to the ceiling. According to US Naval Reserve Ens. William G. Burns, who had been present in the Melody Lounge around that time, the fire began slowly and appeared to be of such a nature that club employees could extinguish it. Suddenly, to everyone's alarm, the fire raced across the ceiling, causing the crowd to scatter for safety.

Within eight minutes of the first sight of flames, the fire, fueled by ample wall and ceiling decorations, had engulfed the entire club, spreading upstairs into the street-level foyer and main dining room. As shouts of "Fire!" rang out while heavy smoke and flames emerged from downstairs, the club lights

---

[*] The fire began in the basement bar, known as the Melody Lounge; it sustained major damage (US Army Signal Corps, Boston Public Library).

went out and panic ensued. US Naval Reserve Lt. John Kip Edwards Jr., who had been upstairs in another of the Grove's lounges and escaped the fire, noted that "it seemed that when the lights went out, everybody's intellect went with them."

Black Smoke, Darkness, and Jammed Doors

Unable to see and increasingly unable to breathe due to the billowing black smoke, patrons stumbled over dining room furniture, frantically searching for a way out of the danger. Amidst the chaos and confusion, many were trampled and crushed, especially because at the club's main exit, a revolving door was jammed after being overwhelmed by the rush of patrons seeking to escape.

A second outlet, consisting of an inward-opening door, effectively became a wall as the panicked crowd pushed forth in an attempt to flee to the streets. Additional exits, if they could be located in the dark, were either blocked or obscured, leaving hundreds trapped within the inferno, desperately hoping for outside rescuers to break through the barriers.

Those unable to escape during the fire's first moments faced little chance of survival, given how rapidly the fire spread and consumed the building. In the end, the conflagration would claim the lives of 492 persons—a count exceeding the building's approved occupancy level. Causes of death were mainly due to asphyxiation and extreme burns sustained from the fire. To this day, the Cocoanut Grove is remembered as the location of the deadliest nightclub fire and second-deadliest single-building fire in American history, only surpassed by a 1903 fire at Chicago's Iroquois Theatre that took 602 lives.*

---

* The duty log from the US Navy Yard notes, "Received call from Boston Police requesting aid in case of the fire at the Cocoanut Grove Night Club" (National Archives, RG 181). View in National Archives Catalog.

Boston firefighting units had responded to the Grove just moments after the blaze began and, almost as quickly, realized the severe, life-threatening nature of the fire and the dire need for additional resources to combat it. Within a forty-five-minute span, Boston's Fire Alarm Headquarters received five alarms, and city officials put out a call for all available ambulances to rendezvous at the night club.

At 10:45 p.m., the Boston Navy yard received that call for aid from the Boston Police Department and immediately mobilized every resource at their disposal. As the duty log notes, the Marine barracks dispatched three trucks manned with five men each, while the yard's medical crew produced six station wagons with drivers and hospital corpsmen. They raced the approximate 3.5-mile route from the Navy yard to the Cocoanut Grove in Bay Village.

Many other military stations within the city and in the surrounding region also responded and rallied personnel to the scene of the fire. Among these were the US Naval Hospital in Chelsea, Massachusetts, which dispatched three ambulances with stretchers, four medical officers, and twelve hospital corpsmen. The US Coast Guard's Shore Patrol dispatched two companies of men with stretchers and trucks, while the Naval Shore Patrol provided sixty men with stretchers and beach wagons. Individual servicemen, who had been in the neighborhood that evening and observed the situation, responded to provide assistance as well.

Military, Civilian Personnel Work to Rescue Victims

Once on-scene, these sailors, Marines, and Coast Guards coordinated with city emergency response personnel to provide crowd control in the immediate vicinity of the nightclub (alongside Army military police units), to break down building exits, to rescue and care for those injured, and to recover the dead.

They systematically formed stretcher lines to remove victims from the still-burning building and to bring them into waiting ambulances for transport to one of the many hospitals throughout the city or, in the case of the deceased, to one of the two city mortuaries.[*]

Describing the magnitude of the work being performed by naval personnel, Lt. Comdr. John J. Reilly of the Naval Shore Patrol recounted that Navy units had removed 165 bodies from the building through one exit alone. Boston's police and fire officials would later compliment the servicemen for their superb work in accomplishing such near-impossible tasks in short order. Reilly recalled Boston Police Capt. James T. Sheehan offering high praise when he stated, "Nothing can take the place of discipline and training. The Navy boys were grand."

In his official report on the fire, Boston Fire Commissioner William Arthur Reilly took note of the "incalculable value" of assistance rendered at the Cocoanut Grove by so many organizations, including the military and civilian defense units located in the Boston area.

While rescue and recovery efforts were ongoing, the First Naval District sought to account for all its personnel and to verify the nature of any serviceman's absenteeism from their duties. According to the Administrative History of the First Naval District in World War II, by early 1943, the district comprised approximately seventeen thousand enlisted men, four thousand officers, and tens of thousands of civilian employees stationed at bases and installations throughout its jurisdiction, stretching from Newfoundland to Newport, Rhode Island.

Accounting for this sizable force spread out across a wide geographic region required keen coordination among the dis-

---

[*] The sheriff's office joined the Boston police and fire departments in commending the US Navy's assistance at the fire and during the recovery (RG 181, National Archives at Boston).

trict's many units. Navy medical staff established temporary posts at the city's civilian hospitals to identify any military personnel who might have been transported there. Those who could be transferred to Chelsea Naval Hospital were moved accord-

ingly so that they could receive the Navy medical resources intended for them while also alleviating the strain on civilian hospitals.

Similarly, the First District assigned personnel to the city mortuaries in order to iden-

tify the bodies of deceased servicemen and to facilitate transfer of their remains to Chelsea Naval Hospital. District intelligence officers also canvassed the hospitals and mortuaries, as well as the scene of the nightclub itself, to ascertain information that might explain how the fire occurred and why so many had perished.

Searches are launched to identify dead, injured.

Military caps lay abandoned, a grim reminder of the many victims of the Cocoanut Grove blaze (Leslie Jones Collection, Boston Public Library).

Numerous dispatches were sent and received between the commandant's office at the Boston Navy Yard and posts throughout New England, seeking to share and obtain information as to the whereabouts and status of absent officers and enlisted men and whether they might have attended the Cocoanut Grove that evening.

At the US naval training school located at Harvard College, officers established a call center to facilitate such communication in order to determine the status of unaccounted for trainees and personnel.

One missing officer, Ens. John Bauer, stationed at the Navy's communication school at Harvard, had not reported for duty during the first three days following the fire. Students at the school informed officers that Bauer had gone to the Cocoanut Grove on Saturday night and feared the worst for him. While

his wallet and uniform cap had been recovered from the nightclub following the fire, his body had not been identified, and companions who might have been able to corroborate Bauer's whereabouts had either died at the Grove that night or were in life-threatening condition in hospitals. Then on December 7, eight days following the disaster, the district's medical corps confirmed that they had identified Bauer's body through dental records and other personal markings on clothing, verifying that his death was a direct result of injuries sustained during the nightclub fire.

Bauer's fate was one of hundreds that would be reported by Boston newspapers as information was learned and disseminated in the days and weeks following the tragedy. On Sunday morning, November 29, the Cocoanut Grove fire dominated the headlines in Boston, and would do so for several days, displacing war updates that normally would have been front page news. Even other big city dailies, such as the *New York Times* and the *Washington Post*, made room on their front pages to report on the events in Boston.

The media printed firsthand accounts of the fire from survivors, eyewitnesses, and emergency responders while publishing lists of the victims, as well as those injured and hospitalized, as such information could be verified. The death of Buck Jones, a popular movie star of the era and attendee at the nightclub, also made national news.

Lord, Thank You for Rescuing My Mother's Life!

What a horrific memory to carry with you in your life, especially when your boyfriend was never found. And I am sure, that was worse than the punishment she got from her mother for secretly leaving the house that dreadful night. Only a parent can know the pain of knowing a child had snuck out and then hearing of the worst fire in Boston's history.

My mother's life changed when she met my dad in 1944 and was married in North Conway, New Hampshire, on July 9 of that year. They lived in a three-floor tenement building on Saratoga Street in East Boston, and she continued to work in the basement at her mother's house, which was right around the corner on Chelsea Street. At least she thought that eventually she could bring her children to work with her because her sister (who was my aunt) lived on the third floor and her older brother (my uncle) lived on the second floor. Also, she had a younger brother, my uncle Tony, who had rheumatic fever, which developed into heart problems, and he also lived on the first floor with my grandmother.

My parents married in 1944 Lawrence
and Rose Drinkwater a/k/a Bevilacqua

My Dad and his twin

crabs 5 cents

Life in East Boston as I can remember was fun as a small child growing up with horse and buggies driving through the streets collecting broken tools, metal, paraphernalia—or junk as they called it—and as they drove they yelled, "Junk, junk," and people would throw it out to them. There were horse and buggies selling crabs for five, ten, or twenty-five cents per bag. You can save your pennies and sit on your front steps for hours cracking the shells and eating succulent chilled crabs. Or you can walk to the corner store and enjoy a paper cup of lemon slush for five cents on a hot summer day. The parades would go by my grandmother's house, and we would sit out front on long benches with all our relatives who came to celebrate the holidays. We loved watching parades at my grandmother's and enjoying her famous Italian cooking. There were always festivities celebrated at her house growing up in East Boston. She made large pots of gravy, as we called it, huge meatballs, fresh homemade sausages, homemade pasta and raviolis and home-baked bread. And all her desserts were homemade Italian pastries. The pleasant aromas drew you to her house, and those were, by far, the best of the good ole days as I remember.

My grandmother actually became quite important when she was asked by her local priest to consider a request from the pope at the Vatican in Italy. My grandmother, being a superb seamstress, was asked by her local priest to design the gown for the statute of the Blessed Mother at the Vatican in Italy. She worked hard and completed the most beautiful and exquisite beaded gown. (see photo) Her family and friends escorted her to Logan Airport with such joy and excitement; and off she went on her journey to Italy with her amazing achievement. It was truly an amazing day and a tribute to my grandma; that was a great memory to treasure forever.

Grandma goes to Italy with her gown for Blessed Mary

Life was not always grand for me though because I can remember living in fear. I was always sick with asthma, doctors constantly making house calls injecting me with penicillin. Finally, they advised my parents to consider moving me out of the city to the North Shore, and to us that sounded like moving to the country. After taking so many penicillin shots and medications, I became severely allergic, and I was told that they almost lost me a few times. So they decided it was time to move out of the city. My life changed for my parents because now with two children and my mother having to stop working with my grandmother, life became more difficult and challenging. But before we were even able to make the move, more pain, suffering, and grief happened as she lost her third child prematurely. I was about four years old when I heard my mom yelling from the bathroom screaming for help. My dad was calling for the neighbor downstairs to call an ambulance and to take me and my sister to her apartment. I ran into the bathroom to see my father filling up a black basin with her blood, and I too started crying.

I can remember that scene like it was yesterday as he kept yelling for us to go downstairs. Meanwhile, my mom was crying out to me and then gave me something and said to run and hide it. I obeyed, not knowing what it was or why. Years later, I learned that she gave me a turquoise ring and a gold locket, and she explained the story to me, which I will share with you later on. I cannot remember if she had those items in her pocket or on her person; I just remember her giving them to me. The ambulance arrived as I ran back into the bathroom, only to see a man stick what looked like a screwdriver into Mommy's heart. I thought, "Now she is dead," as the ambulance took my mom and dad away. I wondered if I would ever see them again. We learned later that my mother lost her son Alfred prematurely. Looking back on those years now, I remember later on asking my mother about the episode of the ring and locket. She told me that they were from her boyfriend Fred, who died at the Cocoanut Grove Fire, and she wanted me to have them so no one would find them. That was when she feared dying that night. The name of her friend was Alfred, but she called him Fred. I never found out if he died, but she believed that he did.

To this day, I have her ring and her locket, which is engraved with both their initials dated 1940, two years before that dreadful fire. I will never forget that memory, and I have her jewelry as a reminder.

Chapter 2

Peabody

Our family in East Boston

My mother survived after losing her son Alfred. Now we were heading to the North Shore in search of our country home away from the city. Our lives changed dramatically in many ways. They bought a house on farmland with a real farm nearby. Living in the country was so different. Grass was almost as high as we were, doors were left unlocked at all times, and there were farm animals running around our house and yard. Pigs and chickens were our closest visitors, sometimes running through our house. And frequently the horses got loose and appeared at our doorstep. I hated the bugs and spiders though, and to this day, I still hate them. My father now had to drive to Boston every day for work, and that pressure and stress affected us all. My sister and I were enrolled in the local elementary school when my brother was born, so we were six years apart. More pressure on my father to work two jobs since my mother could not return to work as she had to care for her new infant son, who was named after my dad. He worked part-time as a chef on weekday evenings and weekends at Bertini's and the Lord Wakefield Restaurants. We often went there for dinner on weekends to see him and always on holidays if and when our relatives drove us there as my mother did not drive. I always remember the delicious raviolis and the homemade Italian bread. To this day, my mouth waters at the thoughts of the delicious food and delicacies and the memories of the holidays spent at those restaurants.

Picture of the farm where I grew up

Myself and my late sister   dancing with brother

We lived on a dead-end road across from woods, quarries, and babbling brooks to explore as we were forever collecting butterflies, pollywogs, frogs, and grasshoppers. Within a year or two, our freedom in the woods was off-limits when a young boy in our neighborhood fell into the quarry and drowned. After a few months, the pain of his loss lessened for us kids, and we became curious again and would sneak off into the woods in search of animals, hidden treasures, and playing hide-and-go-seek. But I do still remember that awful day when he fell into the quarry, and our parents often reminded us so we would stay out of the woods.

Being the only house on the farmland quickly changed when more homes were built, and it became a neighborhood, not a farmland. Fences were put up, so were the rules and regulations to obey. But still, it was a fun place to live with so many kids in the neighborhood that you were never bored. We would play cops and robbers outdoors until dark and the dinner bells would ring—yes, life was good back then. We had pretend marriage ceremonies with the kids in the neighborhood and held pretend church services, playing school and hospital as well. When we played school, we had to alternate who was the teacher or the principal, and whoever were left, they were the students. We really had great kids in the neighborhood, and we enjoyed those days. There were no televisions, no cell phones, and no evil to recall—just fun outdoors riding bikes with neighborhood boys and girls, school days, picnics, drive-in theaters, swimming pools, and playing with our animals.

We had family outings at Stage Fort Park in Gloucester in the summer, and we would go every Saturday and Sunday right after we went to the 7:00 a.m. mass on Sundays. We stopped at the local bakery and always got coffees and donuts for our families. Whoever arrived at the park first would be assigned to collect the picnic tables and join them together for all our Italian relatives. It was so exciting; the parents brought food for the entire day and set up large pots of boiling water for pasta—or we called it macaroni—and gravy. Now people call it sauce and with homemade meatballs and sausages. One of the aunts baked homemade Italian bread, one brought huge pans of fresh garden salad, and another brought plenty of Italian pastries for dessert. Those were the greatest memories I can recall with all my cousins playing softball, whiffle ball, hide-and-go-seek in the rocks, and of course, swimming and diving off the rocks. The park almost always had entertainment after dark like carnival rides, fireworks, and vendors selling all the goodies that kids loved. Those are the days I remember being my favorite time of my childhood life.

Yes, those were the fun days I remember when I was but a child before deceit, fear, and evil started to enter my world. The stress was too much for my dad, I think, because he started to drink every day when he got home from work. They both started smoking cigarettes, which was bad for my asthma condition, like I mentioned earlier. The anger, fighting, outrage, and temper tantrums were horrible. The joy and peace in our home seemed to vanish. The abuse began with my mother, who always feared him as well. I do recall her running away a couple of times and living in the fear of us being left alone with him in that house when she did leave. Thank God she always returned, but she was still afraid of him. Him being a lightweight boxing champion did not help because his hands were so big and he was so strong and muscular that it was scary as a child. I used to think he looked like a guerrilla with dark, tanned skin, and he was full of black hair. He truly scared me. He never missed a day of training and working out. Just his body would bring fear to your bones. Whenever he hit you with those strong hands, you could end up across the room.

The sexual abuse is not an easy topic for me to discuss either. But God has since forgiven me and cleansed me of all sin, unforgiveness, and unrighteousness. Back then though, it seemed that there was a sign engraved on my forehead that said, "Take advantage of me, use me, hurt me, and abuse me." I believe back then I just needed to feel loved and accepted and not rejected. I lived in fear; therefore, I could not discuss this topic with anyone until I went into therapy years later at Salem Hospital. Until then, no one would listen to my plea for help. Prior to that time, I went to a psychologist, who also called himself a pastor, but he took advantage of me. Then I went to a priest for help, but he too wanted to take advantage of me because he said it was safe in the church and no one would know. So that was the end of the Catholic Church for me. The same abuse came when I trusted in another psychologist, and he told me that letting him touch those bad places would make me feel loved and safe. I kept running from all the men I thought who would help me. And then I would feel shame and guilt and depressed, thinking it was always my fault. I just cried all the time, hoping there was someone in this world I could trust and feel safe with. I then thought that love and safety only came if you gave your body to them. Perhaps that psychologist was right, and I began to believe a lie from the devil as they continued to abuse me. Therefore, I held it all in and lived in fear as a victim filled with guilt and shame. Even when we try to hide that pain inside, it eventually shows up, and in my case, it did with a diabetic condition, heart issues, self-destructive behaviors, insomnia, addictions, and anxieties.

The asthma was getting worse, and I could not breathe at times due to the fear in my household and the cigarette smoke. I lived in fear, and I always needed medical care. Just trying to swallow a huge pill was impossible, and that brought anger and abuse from my impatient and angry father. To this very day—more than seventy years later—I still cannot swallow a capsule. He seemed angry at me in all my waking hours. I never could understand why he took everything out on me. I know now. Because they tried to abort me, I lived with rejection. Some of the names I was called were rubber legs, so therefore I always fell. And then it was butter fingers because I always dropped things, and that brought more fear when I dropped anything. I was called stupid and grew up so rejected and sad. I wasn't good at school because I couldn't even think. I feared what would happen if I failed, so I believed therefore that I was stupid. That is the power in words spoken to us. You speak positive words, then you give confidence and love, but I was given negative words which sent me messages of fear, doubt, and rejection. I just could not keep up with life because fear held me back, and the name-calling brought more pain, fear, and rejection. My dad would wake us up at 5:00 a.m. before he left for work by lifting up our mattresses, and we fell onto the cold floor. That was a great way to start your day at school. Our sandwiches were made the night before, and they were always soggy, and the bread was mushy. I still have a difficult time eating sandwiches. If we didn't eat everything on our plates at dinnertime, that would be our breakfast, and if you didn't eat it, then you starved.

My younger brother was a fun-loving brother, and he loved to tease me and my sister a lot. We sure got him back in many ways though. We were always paying him off with our devious secrets and rebellious ways against the rules we had to sustain, like sneaking a boyfriend into the house while my parents were out dancing. Our boyfriends constantly made monetary deals with my brother to keep our secrets. I recall one day when my brother and his friends were playing basketball on this scorching hot summer day. I and my sister made what looked like fruit shakes in the blender filled with all spices, hot sauce, and what looked like juices and crushed ice. They looked so delicious and refreshing, and when we served the boys outside, we immediately ran in the house and locked the doors. When they all gulped that drink down, they were choking and coughing and wanted to kill us—not really, but they almost broke down the door trying to get us. We all had a good laugh, which left us with funny memories to tell even now in our later years! We did need to make excuses why the door was broken though, like someone was trying to break into our house.

My sister and I could not date in high school unless we dated boys together or double-dated, so they had to be friends. Sometimes that was so inconvenient, especially when our dates had to meet his standards. For example, they had to be Catholic, not Jewish, not Greek, and not Irish either. I was always changing their last names. I was dating a Greek guy I really liked, and he played basketball; therefore, his name appeared in the local newspapers whenever he excelled in the game. So I had to bribe the newspaper columnist to add "ski" to his name so my dad thought he was Polish Catholic. Then one week the columnist was not working, and the name of my friend appeared normal. I can still remember the day my father found out he was Greek when he read the paper that morning. So as I and my sister were walking home from school that afternoon with our boyfriends, he pulled over and got out of the car when he saw us and told us to get into the car and yelled at the poor guy to not call on me again. That was the end of that relationship. I was so sad because I really liked him, and now I could not go to the junior prom with him. That really broke my heart; I was so sad about that for years.

Another example of disappointment and deprivation was when I was all dressed and ready for my junior prom and suddenly he would not let me go and canceled it when my date came to the house. I lived with disappointment, frustration, and sadness. I felt deprived and held captive no matter what I did. We were forever doing household chores, homework, and babysitting for my brother so they could go dancing three nights a week. We did sneak in a boyfriend occasionally, like I mentioned, when they were out. But we always got caught, especially if there was a snowfall as the tracks in the snow gave us away. If dinner wasn't on the table when Dad got home from work, he threw the pasta pot of boiling water or a hot pot of coffee that was on the stove across the room, not caring who got hit with it. We all lived in fear, no matter what time of day it was.

One Sunday morning, while getting ready for church, my father yelled to me and my sister to get in the car. But we were still in our underwear and not ready to leave. Rather than being patient so we can continue dressing, he grabbed our heads and banged them together so that our foreheads had an egg-sized bump, and he made us go to church in our underwear with our coats on. So we couldn't even take our coats off in church, which was so embarrassing. If we made a sound, he would pinch our legs or arms so hard we would bruise. Sometimes if I complained to my mother about my dad, she would bite my cheeks, forbidding me to hate my dad. I had teeth marks on my cheeks before going to school. I got it from both of them, and I never felt protected or loved.

I finally turned seventeen years old, and I got my license and was able to go out with my girlfriends without my sister, but with an early curfew. One night we went out to the Caravan

Club in Revere so that I could meet my cousin there to dance and have some fun with her friends from East Boston. When we were leaving the club around ten thirty, we realized that I had a flat tire. I almost passed out crying in fear and begged my friends to help me change the tire. That brought me home a little after midnight. I did try to call my parents from a telephone booth, but they did not answer. Remember, there were no cell phones back then. When I arrived home after taking my friends home, I could see my father in the front large window jumping up and down on the couch like a guerilla. I was actually so scared and weak I could not even walk up the steps to enter the house. He came at me like a maniac, hitting me, banging his head on my forehead, and then hitting me with an empty whiskey bottle. I knew I was bleeding and began yelling how much I hated him. Then my mother started hitting me and telling me not to hate him but that I needed to love and respect him. That was too confusing for me, so I just ran out of the house and got into my car to run away and never come back. I headed to Route 1 and was driving south in the north side lane at a recorded speed of one hundred miles an hour, hoping to die. That was when the police pulled me over and was about to arrest me, but when they saw the blood on my face, they immediately called an ambulance and sent me to the hospital. The doctor looked to me as though he was seven feet tall, and then he had to anesthetize my nose with a syringe up my nostrils in order to break and reset it. I was a mess for sure. I could not tell them the truth with fear that my father would kill me. Later on, when the police went to my house to get my parents, they came to the hospital, and I thought for sure they would love me and apologize. Instead my dad said he was sorry for hurting my beautiful face, but if I came home late again, he would break it even worse. I never could tell anyone the things his bad temper and alcohol did to me. For example, a work shoe was imprinted on my sister's back with a kick that practically knocked her out, sending her down the hall. It was all because my little brother's matchbox car fell in the toilet, which backed it up, flooding the bathroom. But it was not even her fault; she was in the wrong place at the wrong time. I would have been next, but a friend knocked on the door, and I was *rescued*. Must I say more of the horror stories that plagued my childhood? But I could convince myself that it was always my fault due to the guilt, shame, and condemnation I felt. But yes, it is still wrong to abuse anyone, least of all your own children.

My fears grew with the days and years. We did a lot of sneaking around, and we even had to hide our makeup; that was against the rules. But when he found it—and he always did—he would throw it away. He would tell me all the evil things men would do to me, so he would not let me go out. Another time I tried to kill myself by putting a plastic bag from the dry cleaners over my head and tying it. He flipped out when he found me not breathing. I then called my favorite priest, and when he came over to *rescue* me, my father threw him out. He was my favorite priest and friend who, years later, married me and my husband. He baptized my children, and we remained friends until he recently went home to be with the Lord.

I just rebelled and went out to look for love and attention in the wrong places. Anything had to be better than the fear, loneliness, and abuse that I was living in. I ran away many times in my life from those who hurt me, people who held me prisoner in my own fear. There were physical beating, rape, fear, emotional trauma, unhappiness, depression, and loneliness. I thought of so many ways to escape, but there seemed no way out.

I believe a miracle happened which seemed to mellow my father. My mother got pregnant at the age of forty-eight years old. I was taking her to the doctor's office on November 22, 1963, because she was feeling ill for a few weeks. Halfway to the appointment, I got a flat tire. I pulled over, and we prayed for someone to stop and fix my tire since I had no mechanical abilities. And in those days there were no cell phones, so we had to sit and wait for help to appear. Suddenly at 12:45 p.m., an urgent message came on the car radio...

President John F. Kennedy had been assassinated in Dallas, Texas, while riding in a presidential motorcade through Dealey Plaza. As you know, he was the thirty-fifth president of the United States. We screamed and cried, and we were so upset we forgot about the flat tire. Finally, a nice guy stopped, and we were all crying over this news. After he so kindly fixed my tire, we took off to her appointment. She came out of the office to tell me that she was two months pregnant. We were sad and happy at the same time, and now she had to go home and tell my dad the news. I can still see him sitting in our small, child-sized rocking chair so upset while watching the news.

We said, "Ma's pregnant, Dad," and he jumped up, but he was stuck in the chair. We could not stop laughing and yet crying at the same time. That day is locked into my memory forever. My younger sister was born less than eight months later, weighing over ten pounds. That blessed event really started to mellow my dad, and finally it brought joy and peace to our family.

After high school, my sister was enrolled in Perry Winkle School in Boston for early childhood education, and I was almost eighteen. Soon I would graduate from high school. I did miss my sister so much as I had to go through my senior year without her. That was hard since we always had to go out together, so her friends were my friends, and now they were gone. I felt abandoned and had to make new friends for myself, and that was frightening. Funny thing is, though, I did well, and I was even voted the vice president of my class. So I did enjoy my senior year after all.

My sister met her husband and dropped out of college to get married. That was even more difficult for me when she moved away and left our house.

I worked in a dental office near my home when I was sixteen, and the dentist sent me to Northeastern part time where I graduated as a certified dental assistant. I then became his office manager and continued working for him for a couple of years before marrying my husband. Sad to say, though, that bad things started to happen to me while I was working for that dentist. He began using "laughing gas," or nitrous oxide, to work on my teeth, and I recall when he said I had so many cavities that I did not want to believe him back then. Now I questioned that I probably did not, and that made me sad. I later realized that he started to take advantage of me during those treatment times. I did not face that truth until many years later while going to counseling and therapy. I realized the truth when I ran into the dentist at the gym years later. He recognized me and came over to hug me and gave me a kiss; his breath hit a strong note in my heart, and I became nauseous and furious, and I didn't know why I was reacting that way. The smell of his breath brought back horrific memories that I needed to share with my doctors at Salem Hospital immediately. When I brought up those feelings and the memories to my next appointment, the team of psychiatrists confirmed the abuse from the dentist. They believed that the pain and suffering that I have buried from my childhood was the result of diabetes and other conditions I have had to deal with. The realization of facing that truth was very painful, and I had to forgive the dentist of the pain and shame that he caused me in my early years. I eventually visited him so that I could forgive him, and he died soon thereafter of a heart attack.

I met my soon-to-be husband at my cousin's wedding at age nineteen. We became friends instantly, and he often came to my house to visit me. My parents liked him very much. He was a student at Boston University studying aeronautical engineering, and after his graduation, we became engaged. However, he did know how my dad treated me as he witnessed a few of his outbursts, and he felt bad for me and wanted to get me out of the abusive environment so I could start a new life. It was very exciting for me to finally escape. We set a wedding date, shopped for my gown, found a hall for the reception, and made all the necessary wedding arrangements. Within a month before the wedding date, his parents called it off because they were going to France. We thought that was strange, and I actually couldn't believe that they would take a vacation when our wedding date was already set. Well, that was another blow to me as I had my gown custom-made, down payments were made on the restaurant, invitations were ready to mail, and I was devastated. To keep peace, we scheduled another date, and that too was soon canceled due to another excuse from his parents. So my family invited his family to our house to find out why they kept canceling the wedding date. They told my parents they preferred that their son marry his own kind, preferably an Armenian. Then they wanted to see my health records to be sure their future grandchildren would be healthy and disease-free. My father was not happy and got quite angry and commanded them to leave. So after they canceled wedding dates, we secretly eloped to New York. More rejection, more pain, and more suffering tormented me because I could not understand why his family rejected me. Because I was not Armenian? But I was a human being that loved their son, who protected me and wanted me to be his wife.

I recently did some research about the genocide and how the Armenians suffered and overcame by their faith and strength in God. My father-in-law saw his family brutalized and killed right before his eyes by the Turks, but I just wished they told me about their heritage and suffering, so then I could have understood their anger and rejection. All those years I spent thinking they rejected me, only to find out years later that their anger was toward the Turks, who persecuted their family. I just wanted them to love and accept me and not treat me like an outsider. I also found out later that Armenia was the first sovereign nation to accept Christianity as a state religion. Eventually, Eastern Armenia was conquered by Russia in nineteenth century, and in the twentieth century, Armenians suffered in that horrific genocide where 1.5 million Armenians were killed. But praise God that they regained independence in 1991 as the Republic of Armenia. I could have been saved years of pain, sin, and suffering had I understood the pain and suffering they endured in their lifetime.

However, I had a good relationship with Grandma Acaby and her children who really loved me, and I loved them as well. I adored Grandma Acaby. She was the sweetest woman I had ever met. Also, I felt loved by my father-in-law, who was so kind, gentle, and loving toward me. Years later, he turned ill, and he was diagnosed with cancer, which was so surprising since he was a very healthy man. God put it on my heart one day to visit him in the hospital and pray with and for him. I remember that day like it was yesterday. I prayed in my car for grace and love to fill me and that no one would be in the room so that I could share Jesus Christ with him. When I entered his room, all the family had left, and I sat beside his bed, held his hand, and we shared Jesus Christ as we both were filled with love and shed many tears. Then he took an old, tattered, and torn pamphlet about the love of Jesus Christ from his pajama pocket. He told me he kept that pamphlet and read it every day for years since the day I gave it to him, which was years ago. We held each other, and he asked me to always pray for his family when he went to his heavenly home so that one day we would all spend eternity together in heaven. I made that promise to him, and I have kept it since that day. I remember he gave me his cashmere overcoat, which I would wear in the winter months even though it was a man's coat, and it just reminded me that he was watching over me. The coat even had the sales slip for $2,000 from Filene's Basement in the pocket. I needed to remember him and his love for me. I have since given it to my first grandson to wear so he could remember his great-grandfather who loved his family so much. My father-in-law was soon escorted to his heavenly home shortly thereafter.

When my son got married in September 2001, I was able to make peace with my mother-in-law at my son's wedding when I forgave her for making my life so difficult and for not accepting me as her son's wife. She wept before me and asked me to forgive her and told me that she had always loved me. I asked her why she never told me that back then or why I wasn't good enough for her son. She just wept with sorrow in her heart. She did pray with me that day as she accepted Jesus Christ as her Lord and Savior. I thanked God with all my heart for keeping the promise to my father-in-law to pray for all of his family. I still pray for the family, and I truly believe that we will all meet one day and enjoy fellowship with our Lord and Savior for all of eternity. I do still have a close relationship with the family, and I will always love and respect them for being so wonderful to my children.

When we returned from our wedding in New York, our parents decided we should have a large wedding, and they planned a shower followed by a wedding on October 21. I then found out I was pregnant and I was due in June the following year. I had my son on June 9, and we moved to Windsor Locks, Connecticut, where my husband got his first job after graduating from Boston University. We planned our son's baptism at a Catholic Church we were attending and invited my old friend and priest, the late Pastor Bourgeois, to officiate the ceremony. However, while we were driving to the Catholic Church, the driver took a different route to an Armenian Church, of which I knew nothing about. I was so hurt and upset again that we had an Armenian ceremony without my knowledge. I recall my in-laws telling my husband that we had to bring the children up in the Armenian Church or my husband would lose his inheritance. Thank God that statement never came to pass. I recall always feeling rejected by his family, which brought more lies, sadness, and rejection to my life. I only wish I knew then what I know now about the Armenians and how they suffered and endured, and perhaps we would have had a better ending to this story. I do thank God that all is forgiven and we are a very happy family to this day.

We loved family parties where everyone loved to dance

Dad dancing with his Mom

Parents dancing

My baby sister was born

Chapter 3

Wakefield

I did miss my immediate family while living in Windsor Locks, Connecticut, so after a couple of years, we decided to move back to Massachusetts, and we settled in Wakefield, Massachusetts. I thought the reason for my depression was because I missed my family. We rented the second-floor apartment in Wakefield from an elderly Jewish couple. They were very nice, and our apartment was clean and a blessing. The only thing I hated was that the Jewish cooking always made me ill. I hated the fact that the entire apartment would smell the odors of whatever they prepared for dinner. It became almost intolerable for me. We had great neighbors, and we truly enjoyed the neighborhood though.

A funny story I remember happened one early morning while my husband and I were still sleeping. Our son, who was extremely active, ran out of the house and took the skeleton key and locked the back door when he left the house. When we awoke and could not find him anywhere, we panicked, especially when we could not even leave the house to look for him. We had to call the local police to report him missing, and when we finally got out through the front door, the police were there to help in the search. He was so full of energy, but we never considered that he would lock the door so we could not get out. The police found him riding the swings at the local playground that was adjacent to our yard. He even climbed the fence to get to the park, and he was not even two and a half years old. He was so active that we had to bar the bedroom windows so he would not jump out. For example, he climbed out of his crib at age one, so he was in a youth bed soon thereafter.

At age one, my son got sick with an ear infection and was on penicillin for a couple of weeks with no sign of healing. We called his pediatrician several times to report that his condition was not improving and he had a high fever. I will never forget when the doctor told us to put cotton in our ears, close his door, and let him cry and that we were spoiling him. We were so upset that we immediately took him to Boston Children's Hospital.

When we got to the emergency room the doctor on duty said to us, "Were you waiting to put him in a box?"

We were mortified after what our pediatrician said to us— to put cotton in our ears—earlier that day. They had to fly several doctors to Boston to diagnose his condition while he was in quarantine, and I couldn't even hold my son to comfort him. He was then diagnosed with Stevens-Johnson syndrome, which is an allergic reaction to a drug, and in his case, that was penicillin. He was hospitalized for a few weeks during the Christmas holiday, and his body was actually bleeding internally as well as externally. At that time, it was the seventh case of that condition reported in the United States. Because of that disease, his body was scarred as well. That year we had to celebrate Christmas holiday after the New Year. We found a Christmas tree on the side of the road and took it home to decorate it before he came home. That was a sad holiday that year, but the good news was that he got healed, and we had lots to be grateful for. He was toilet-trained and drank from a cup and fed himself. Before he got sick, I was still breastfeeding him. He became so independent and grown up. He has always been bright and intelligent—a wonderful, caring, loving, and faithful son, father, and husband who has blessed me with two amazing and beautiful grandchildren and a lovely daughter-in-law. They are great parents to our grandchildren and we are so blessed.

Then my beautiful daughter was born, and a new journey of my life began. As a baby, she could not hold down any milk but vomited after every feeding, and she was losing weight. The doctor diagnosed it as a hole in her stomach and said she needed immediate surgery. We decided to call our parish priest and have her baptized the next day at our home. After the baptism, the pastor prayed a prayer of healing over her, and we felt confident that all would be well for her. The next day we went to the children's hospital, and she was admitted for surgery. While waiting for her in the waiting room, the doctor came out sooner than expected, with our daughter in his arms and the good news that she did not need surgery because there was no hole. Of course, we were so excited, and that was my first real test of faith, and I didn't even have a personal relationship with Jesus at that time. I knew there was a God, and we went to church, but I never had a real loving relationship with Jesus Christ as I do now. Nor did I know that you could pray to God for a healing. She has grown up to be an incredible young woman who is a kind, loving, and caring daughter, wife, and mother of two great and awesome grandchildren. She is married to a wonderful man who is a great son-in-law and provider for his family. We are so thankful and blessed.

We finally moved from the apartment, and we bought a house on the other end of the playground on Harrington Court. (I think that was why I was always sick with the smells of the Jewish food from downstairs filling the house with odors that made me ill, because I was pregnant.) The new house was a fixer-upper, and my husband chose to remodel it. He was so handy, but he still worked full-time at General Electric and worked nights and weekends to remodel the house. I will never forget when he cut off his finger with the electric saw in the basement, and I always felt that it was my fault. He went through so many surgeries to attach his finger back to his hand. It was just so sad and ugly, and I blamed myself for those injuries. If I hadn't called him to hurry up because we had a dinner engagement to attend, that accident would not have happened. We were no longer happy in that new house, so we decided to sell it, make our profit, and move out to a newer house. We found a beautiful center entrance colonial home in Melrose; we sold the fixer upper and made a great profit.

Son and his dad
and grandpa

Son with his family

Daughter as a baby

Daughter and her family

Chapter 4

Melrose

Our new home had three bedrooms, two baths, and a finished family room in the basement. It was perfect with a deck and a great fenced-in yard. The kids were coming from a dead-end street adjacent to a park and playground to a busy street with rules and boundaries to obey. We made new friends and enjoyed the golf course across the street. I could walk there in the morning before the golfers went out, and the kids could play there after golfer's hours. We were able to sled down the hills in the wintertime and walk around it in the spring and summer. My son loved to search for golf balls in the small ponds or water hazards, and he would clean them up, put them in baggies, and then sell them in front of our house by passersby who would stop for the bargains. He made some extra spending money as well. I got a job at a local day care center, which was only a few houses down the street, and my kids could walk there after school. They were a great help for the teachers with the after-school projects, plus I could keep an eye on them while I was working.

As I mentioned earlier, I was trained as a dental assistant when I worked in my neighborhood during my high school years for a dentist. During those years, he sent me to Northeastern in Boston, where I got my certificate as a certified dental assistant. That came in handy, so I could work in the evenings for a local dentist when my husband got home from his job at General Electric. We led busy lives, as most parents did, with our children's sports and activities.

I knew I needed to continue to seek counseling so that I would do a better job in parenting than what I learned from my parents. I needed to know how to love and forgive those who hurt me. I wanted to break that curse over my life. The church offered a weekend seminar called "*Healing and Forgiveness*," and I decided to attend. I cried all that weekend because I could not forgive my parents and those who hurt me. The counselors advised me to ask God and He would love and forgive them through me. They said to beware of a hardened heart. It could cause me to forget what God can do for me and how He could set me free. But who was this God they all talked about, and how do I have a relationship with Him? The counselor advised me to visit my dad after the seminar and ask him to forgive me. I thought that was strange and outrageous because my parents should ask me to forgive them for all they had done to me, especially my father. And why didn't my mother protect me? But after crying and feeling all the pain again, I agreed to visit my dad after the seminar because it was his sixty-first birthday. When I entered the room, I ran over to him, and I was very emotional. I asked him to forgive me like the counselor advised me to.

He was shocked and asked, "Why?"

I said, "For hating you in all the years that you hurt me."

He broke down in my arms and asked me to forgive him for all that he had done to me. We both cried as we embraced each other with love. He asked God to forgive him as well, and I believe that the counselor's advice was successful.

Two weeks later, while my husband and I and our kids were off to Disney World, I got a call that my father suddenly died of a severe heart attack. I was a mess to say the least. I became so angry at God, and I could not believe that He would take my father away from me after giving him to me to love and be loved.

That's when I went further away from a God, who I thought hurt me just like men always did. We had to fly back immediately to attend the services and to now take care of my grieving mother. More fear and bitterness set in on an already-hardened heart.

However, I was still having problems in my life and blamed it on my marriage. Now I can see God was trying to get my attention to invite Jesus into my life and fill that hole in my heart that just wanted to be loved. I was not happy with myself even though we did have some great years together as a family. We took trips to Cape Cod every summer; we went to Disney World in Florida and Disney Land in California; and we made the best of our marriage even though I was a broken child in a grown-up body.

Although I was married, I did not feel free. I was a broken woman who was depressed and unhappy. I desperately needed healing because of the memories that always haunted me. I needed to address my pain and go back into therapy. Please know that I loved and admired my husband for taking me away from the abuse, and I love him to this very day. I will always be grateful and thankful for all he did for me. To date, we are great friends, and he is a wonderful father and grandfather. But at that time, my heart ached because I was missing something, and I could not fill that hole in my heart or ease the pain and torment I lived in. I thought the only thing to make things better was to divorce my husband because I was such a mess, so that was what I did. My anger was hidden deep within me for all the men that abused me. I told my husband I could no longer live like that. I needed more time, or maybe I just needed to live alone so I could escape the guilt I felt and the anger toward God and man. We were divorced, and that really was not the wisdom from God, I learned later on. My life only got worse.

I began to search in the wrong places for love and attention. When I filed for a divorce, I thought I would find freedom and peace. Looking back now, I can see how wrong and deceived I was. I realize now I made a terrible mistake. I became a bartender. I started drinking alcohol, hanging with the wrong crowds, and taking drugs to ease my pain. I was searching to fill that hole in my heart like I mentioned earlier, but they were all dead ends. I left the teaching career after my father passed away because my boss wouldn't give me two days off to attend my dad's services, and I truly needed that time to grieve. So he fired me, and that was it for men disappointing me—or at least that was how I felt at that time. I needed to grieve!

I got a job as a secretary for a hypnotist in Everett, and I allowed him to use me for all his demonic tricks, thinking that it was part of the training. That only led me to more pain when he had me studying transcendental meditation, witchcraft, devils and demons, and then astral projection. He hypnotized me often, and my body would levitate as well. It was all pretty interesting at first, and then it became very scary. But like I said, I was searching for peace in the wrong places, and the enemy was controlling me in the worst way! I was far from being godly. One day, as his secretary, I found a marriage certificate in his desk with both our names on it and a future wedding date. I never had a personal or sexual relationship with that man either. So I was horrified to the point of being sick. I told him I wanted out and quit the job, and he held a gun to my head, telling me I would marry him, or else he would kill me. I flipped over some chairs to trip him as I ran out of his office as fast as I could. He then loosed his two Doberman dogs after me. I ran with a strength and speed that I couldn't believe I even had or knew where it came from. It was by the grace of God, with Whom I did not yet have a personal relationship that I was able to escape. It was a miracle in itself. I got home and locked all the doors and ran upstairs and grabbed the crucifix off my bedroom wall. Then he arrived at my house, banging on the door, but I courageously held a crucifix of Jesus Christ and called on

Jesus's name to the back door window where he was knocking. He finally gave up, and I never saw or heard from him again. I remembered that my girlfriend told me to hold up a crucifix if ever I was in trouble. She said, "Call on the NAME OF JESUS." Well, it worked, and that was when I began thinking about who this man called JESUS is?

> There is no one like the God of Israel. He rides across the heavens to help you, across the skies in majestic splendor. The eternal God is your refuge, and his everlasting arms are under you. He drives out the enemy before you; he cries out, "Destroy them!" (Deuteronomy 33:26–27)

On and on, I went in search for love, freedom, peace, and joy. I smoked weed, was introduced to cocaine, uppers and downers, you name it I tried it. When I was introduced to Heroin is when God put a stop to my drugs and began to deal with me. Those avenues only brought me more despair, more pain, more abuse, more loss, and eventually losing custody of my two children. That horrified me the most, and anger welled up inside of me to continue to blame and hate men. When two policemen came into my house and took my children out of my arms, I thought for sure I would die. Custody was taken away from me, and I hated men even more. To get deeper in debt, I got involved with a drug dealer I met while working at the restaurant. My plan was to steal some drugs and eventually kill myself because I no longer wanted to live. How does a mother want to live without the love of her children, only to feel the guilt and pain of her broken heart every day? I had enough of this life of guilt, shame, anger, bitterness, and hatred.

One night, during a party at his house, Mr. Drug Dealer drugged me, and he and several of his friends raped me. He told me that his dead wife was a witch, and she did not want me dating her husband. Therefore, the demons would torment me, and that they did all night. I remember when the windows opened and shut, red-eyed demons torturing me, pictures on the walls moving up and down and, some even falling off the walls. They were torturing me beyond my belief. He told me the demons wanted to kill me, and by now, I believed him. I recall sitting in a corner in the fetal position crying out for help. I even called on God to help me, like many people so often do when they are in trouble! I sure needed help more than ever, and I called on God to set me free.

Suddenly, a man entered the room, and he was so gentle and kind. To this day, I often wonder if he was an angel sent by God to *rescue* me after my final cry for help. Rather than rape me, he took off his coat and wrapped me in it and carried me out of the house and drove me home. He left me at my doorstep, and I swear it was a "God moment" for me.

The very next night, I felt so ashamed, so ugly, and so guilty. I could not see my way out of this darkness; my sins overwhelmed me. I felt chained with no escape or ability to break loose. It was time to end the abuse, the drugs, and the men who had always hurt me. I decided that this was the day to surrender my life and take the pills I confiscated from the drug dealer. I could feel Satan's hand trying to choke me, and I could not breathe. I dumped the pills I saved on the kitchen table in front of me and was about to swallow them when I stopped and screamed one last time…*"If there is a God, please rescue me because this time I am killing myself."* The next thing I remember was the front door mail slot opening and an unmarked white envelope slipping through the door slot. I put the pills down. I looked out the window to see who could have dropped it off, but the night was black, and there was not a soul in sight. It was a sealed, blank white envelope. I opened it to find a poem called *"Footprints."*

FOOTPRINTS

One night a man had a dream. He dreamed he was walking along the beach with the LORD. Across the sky flashed scenes from his life. For each scene, he noticed two sets of footprints in the sand; one belonged to him, and the other to the LORD.

When the last scene of his life flashed before him, he looked back at the footprints in the sand. He noticed that many times along the path of his life there was only one set of footprints. He also noticed that it happened at the very lowest and saddest times in his life.

This really bothered him and he questioned the LORD about it. "LORD, you said that once I decided to follow you, you'd walk with me all the way. But I have noticed that during the most troublesome times in my life, there is only one set of footprints. I don't understand why when I needed you most you would leave me."

The LORD replied, "My precious, precious child, I love you and I would never leave you. During your times of trial and suffering, when you see only one set of footprints, it was then that I carried you."

As I began to read it, I could not stop crying. "Who is this *Jesus?*" I cried. "Who are you?" I yelled.

Then a bright light looking like the sun appeared in the room, blinding me so I could not even see. As the *light* came closer to me, I backed away until there was nowhere else to go, and I fell on the floor against the refrigerator. As the *light* continued to shine on me, a small, still voice kept saying, *"I love you, Carol…you cannot kill yourself because you belong to Me. You are My beloved daughter, and I am your Father, and you are Mine."*

That's when I saw the *light* that was blinding me! The Lord Himself ministered to me with a love I have never experienced from any human being on this earth. It was a love so tender, so kind, so warm, so forgiving, and so loving. It seemed as though I was crying for hours, for days, and for weeks, getting to know this God Who *rescued me* and loved me. He told me to find a Bible and read the book of St. John. I found one and spent days reading and talking to my Jesus. He then showed me a huge warehouse, and it was filled with pictures of the people that abused me, raped me, rejected me, hurt me, and I could not stop crying. He revealed to me all my sins and the horrors of abuse and pain. I was so ashamed, guilty, and fearful.

"No," He said to me. "I come to heal you and to set you free." He covered me with His robe of righteousness and said, "Be ye cleansed, my daughter, I love you!"

I cried out in pain as He ministered to me, suturing the wounds of my broken heart. He told me that I needed to forgive all of the people that harmed me and who stole my childhood. He said I needed to forgive them so that He could forgive me. That is the only way that He could plant the seed of love in my heart. He said it would be like a thorn that would hurt going in, but then it would produce for Him a beautiful rose with a scent that would be a sweet-smelling fragrance to His nostrils. He said I must trust Him, and He would forgive and love them through me, but I must trust Him. Finally, after weeks of deliverance from the pains of abuse and rejection, I began to feel free as if He broke the prison gates and cut apart the bars that held me captive for all those years. Jesus became my Lord and Savior, and the chain-breaker Who led me from a dark dungeon of death and broke every chain that held me bound. I could now live a life of love. I will love Jesus for all eternity, and I thank Him every day for this new life in Him.

> Lord my God, I called to you for help, and you healed me. You, Lord, brought me up from the realm of the dead; you spared me from going down to the pit. (Psalm 30:2–3)
>
> Your arm is endowed with power; your hand is strong, your right hand exalted. Righteousness and justice are the foundation of your throne; love and faithfulness go before you. Blessed are those who have learned to acclaim you, who walk in the light of your presence, LORD. They rejoice in your name all day long; they celebrate your righteousness. (Psalm 89:13–16)

Friend Stef brought me to the Lord

For once He destroyed Satan who was holding me captive. So now I ask my Lord if I can share the *light* so others will know His great grace! He told me weeks later to call the Lord's Gathering Church and get baptized. I knew about the church through friends who attended there. In fact, I hired a teacher when I worked as a coordinator at that local nursery school a few years back. Her name was Ms. Stef. She was a Christian, and when I hired her years ago, she always tried to tell me about her Jesus, but I would not listen. She would always tell me that my house was built on sand and it was falling apart quickly. But I would not believe her or understand her, so I avoided her at all costs. She would tell me that I needed to build my house on the Rock. Jesus Christ, the Rock of Zion, is His name. You see, God had not removed the scales from my eyes, nor did he unblock my ears to hear His words of love and truth at that time. But after I invited Jesus Christ into my life and got baptized, I asked

Him to forgive me of my sins. Then my eyes were opened, and I believed! I later found out that her friends from the church were called together at midnight that night of my suicide attempt to pray for me; the Lord told them that I was going to take my life that night. They were so obedient and prayed for me until 4:00 a.m. After my baptism, they shared that story with me, and I praised God with a grateful heart of thanksgiving. For God who said, "Let there be light in the darkness," has made this light shine in our hearts so we could know the glory of God that is seen in the face of Jesus Christ (2 Corinthians 4:6).

Yes, I did call the church as God told me to, and I got baptized on August 14, 1979. While the pastor was trying to immerse me into the water, I was so fearful that it took twenty minutes to convince me to get dunked. One day I had almost drowned when my father threw me into a pool for fun, which ended up being an almost-tragic event when the fire department was called to *rescue* me. When the pastor told me that my sins would be like an oil slick in the river never to be seen again, I finally allowed him to baptize me. When I came up, I received the Holy Spirit, and I began praying in tongues. I had no clue what that was, but the onlookers and friends were all yelling, "She received the Holy

Spirit, praise God." My life changed at that moment, and I was set free at last. I actually swam to the dock, which I was never able to do, and I praised my God and Savior Jesus Christ.

He led me from the darkness and deepest gloom; He snapped my chains. Hallelujah (Psalm 107:14).

After the miracle of my salvation, I decided to get more serious and continued to seek professional help. As the pains of suffering from my past continued to torment me with nightmares, I agreed to accept an offer from my primary care physician to start a healing program with three top psychiatrists at Salem Hospital. That was the most difficult time of healing for me. They brought all my past hurts in the open so that I could feel the pain and forgive my tormentors—for instance, like the dentist I worked for. Then they invited my mother to join some of these healing sessions so that I could forgive her and go on with my life. I relived many of the painful circumstances in my life, and I was able to feel the pain again and forgive. My mother was also able to receive healing and deliverance. By this time, my father had already died, but I still needed to go to the cemetery and continue my healing work with him by faith. This was when my mom confessed her pain and sorrow for what she had allowed to happen to me, and I needed to forgive her as well. These were very difficult times for me, but the cleansing finally set me free, and I was able to restore a relationship with my mother and with myself freeing myself of guilt, condemnation, and shame. I was now able to work to get healed, as she did the same, and I had to forgive her for wanting to abort me at conception.

Thankfully, I had a loving God Who wanted to *rescue* me and set me free. A God Who loved me so tenderly, Who created me in His image and likeness, a God Who sent His only begotten Son to be the propitiation for my sins, the scapegoat Who died so that I could live. But I kept turning away from His love because I still feared men. How could I trust Him and accept that love when I never knew love? I only knew a father whom I feared, a father who abused me, a father who hurt me since childhood, and a mother who did not protect me. I had parents who did not plan to have another child at that time and who tried to abort me on three occasions. But why was I still alive. Why then did this so-called God keep me alive for all these years? This I needed to find out… Who is this God of love that saved me and set me free?

> For you were once darkness, but now you are light in the Lord. Live as children of light. (Ephesians 5:8)

I made a commitment to search the scriptures to know… who is this loving God that saved me and how do I have a deeper relationship with Him? That was when my life began to change. I did not want to even leave my house; I wanted to read the Bible and discover Who God was and how He could love me so much that He would send His only begotten Son to be the scapegoat and take my sins upon himself and die on a cross for me. The more I read, the more I kept falling in love with Him. I could feel His love as He spoke to me in His Word. I could not stop crying day after day because I never knew or felt a love so great like that in my heart. I felt protected like never before. I sang songs of joy and peace, which would flood my soul with love. I kept reading and singing to HIM… When my friends came to the door with the bottle of booze and the drugs, I wouldn't even answer the door. I let the Lord love me, teach me His Word, and hold me in His loving arms day in and day out. I was truly in love for the first time in my life, and I would not allow anything or anyone to take that from me. Yes, I missed my children, but God even changed that situation for me. I later went to court, and I got back custody of my children, and that was the second greatest miracle of my life. They were so happy to see the change in me that they too wanted to know my Jesus, and they were later baptized and joined the family of God.

> And we know that God causes everything to work together for the good of those who love God and are called according to his purpose for them. (Romans 8:28)

Put on the Armor of God Daily

Armor of God

Here is another reason I needed to know God's Word and learn about the armor of God.

It was a warm Friday evening about 6:00 p.m. when I decided to go to a prayer meeting in Malden while the kids were out to dinner with their dad. Rather than drive, I wanted to take my bike and enjoy the weather and my newfound freedom. Little did I know, it would be a challenge I needed to overcome. I stopped at the corner store on Main Street to get a pack of gum, and there was a man standing out front who said, "What is a young woman like you doing riding your bike while darkness is approaching?"

I became offended rather than thankful, and I answered him with pride and arrogance. I told him it was not his business and I was now a born-again Christian and I knew that God would take care of me. Looking back at that event now, I think it could have been an angel watching out for me, but I did not heed the warning. Because at 10:30 p.m., while riding home that night, a pickup truck approached me, riding too close to my body for comfort. I actually felt the truck wisp by my legs and bike when suddenly they stopped the truck and two men grabbed me off of my bike and threw me onto the bed of the truck. The only thing I could remember at that moment was the NAME OF JESUS that it was confirmed at the Bible study I was returning home from. So I called loudly the NAME OF JESUS, and I yelled it again and again until they tossed me out of the truck and sped away in the night. Yes, I was fearful as I lay on the ground, but thankful to be free and that my bike was still in good-enough condition to ride it home. But I sure was weak and frightened more than ever. The tools God gave me to learn that night: *THERE IS POWER IN THE NAME OF JESUS* and *I OVERCAME* by the *BLOOD OF THE LAMB AND THE WORDS OF MY TESTIMONY*! I believe today that our testimonies are learning experiences, and as Christians we must overcome and stand strong in Him and in His mighty power. God said that the same power that raised Christ from the dead lives in us; therefore, we can do all things through Him who strengthens us. For without a test, there is no testimony! Without the mess, there is no message to tell of the mighty acts of Jesus Christ.

God is teaching me to trust and to obey Him. In order to do that, I had to learn that there is an enemy who wants to take me back to his realm of sin, hatred, and evil. So it was imperative that I learned how to put on the full armor of God as described in chapter 6 of the book of Ephesians. We must be strong in Him and fight this good fight of faith, by dying to self and walking with Him. He will lead and guide me in His perfect will for my life, and His grace is sufficient for me. I must trust Him knowing that the enemy comes to kill, steal, and destroy us. God came to give us life and life more abundantly (John 10:10)! My prayer is that more men and women would join the army of the Living God and stand at the wall and fight for this world to set the captives free, to heal the sick and the brokenhearted, so they too could enter the kingdom of God. I realized now that I have been called to join the army of the Living God. And to be the intercessor He has called me to be, I will not be living on a cruise ship, but now I will live on God's battleship to fight the good fight "of faith" and win souls for Him!

> When I think of all this, I fall to my knees and pray to the Father, the Creator of everything in heaven and on earth. I pray that from his glorious, unlimited resources he will empower you with inner strength through his Spirit. Then Christ will make his home in your hearts as you trust in him. Your roots will grow down into God's love and keep you strong. And may you have the power to

understand, as all God's people should, how wide, how long, how high, and how deep his love is. May you experience the love of Christ, though it is too great to fully understand. Then you will be made complete with all the fullness of life and power that comes from God. (Ephesians 3:14–20)

I have realized that life can ambush us with overwhelming challenges, yet our fears and uncertainties give us the opportunity to turn to our all-powerful God. He is the source of our strength and peace, and He encourages me as I wait for Him to intervene on my behalf. He is not predictable, but He is always unfailingly reliable.

LORD, sustain me as you promised that I may live! Do not let my hope be crushed. Sustain me, and I will be rescued; then I will meditate continually on your decrees. Praise the LORD. (Psalm 119:116–117)

Praise the LORD, all you nations; extol Him, all you peoples. For great is His love toward us, and the faithfulness of the LORD endures forever. Praise the LORD. (Psalm 117:1)

• God Is Teaching Me Obedience

God is teaching me to hear His voice and to obey Him. And the testimonies became more real to me, and I know now why He told me that I would be the pen of the ready writer. Because without the tests, there are no testimonies! He said to me that He knows the plans that He has for me to prosper me and not to harm me, and He has plans to give me hope and a future. He told me that when I pray to Him, He will always listen, and when I seek Him with all of my heart, I will find him. Hallelujah!

> "For I know the plans I have for you," says the LORD. "They are plans for good and not for disaster, to give you a future and a hope. In those days when you pray, I will listen. If you look for me wholeheartedly, you will find me. I will be found by you," says the LORD. "I will end your captivity and restore your fortunes. I will gather you out of the nations where I sent you and will bring you home again to your own land." (Jeremiah 29:11–13)

- God Is Teaching Me Obedience for Tithing

I recall the first church service my friends took me to back in 1979. The message that day was on tithing, and I did not even know what the word meant. I had just recently got custody back of my two children, and this would now be a common thing to do on Sunday mornings… We would go to church and get to know the God Who saved us from our sins and the evil of my past life. The pastor was teaching us how to give back to God and to pay your tithes every week. I wasn't working at that time, and I had only five dollars in my wallet. In fact, the plan was to go to the store after church and buy what we needed like bread, milk, and peanut butter. I had not yet received alimony from my husband now that I got custody for my kids, so I did not have any money. I trusted God with my salvation, the forgiveness of my sins, and baptizing me and my children who now accepted Jesus as their Lord and Savior. But giving the Lord money was something new that I needed to understand. He taught from Malachi

3:8–10, and after the service, I told the kids I needed to give that $5 in my wallet to God in thanksgiving for all He has done for us.

> Should people cheat God? Yet you have cheated me! "But you ask, 'What do you mean? When did we ever cheat you?' You have cheated me of the tithes and offerings due to me. You are under a curse, for your whole nation has been cheating me. Bring all the tithes into the storehouse so there will be enough food in my Temple. If you do," said the LORD of Heaven's Armies, "I will open the windows of heaven for you. I will pour out a blessing so great you won't have enough room to take it in! Try it! Put me to the test!" (Malachi 3:8–11)

So I decided to put God to the test like He said in His Word, and I placed the only $5 into the wooden box at the back of the church. My kids were not happy and wondered what we would do for food. They began to argue in the car, and I told them that we just need to pray and ask God to double our blessing so that we could eat that day. We went home and sat around the table as my children argued as to what they could eat. While arguing, my son tipped over the sugar bowl that was on the table, and out of it was a $10 bill. We all screamed in astonishment and excitement and wondered how it got in the sugar bowl. Well, we didn't wait long to figure it out but thanked God with all our heart and got in the car to the grocery store. We purchased bread, milk, jelly, and peanut butter, and the bill came to $9.94. We could not stop praising God, and that night the Lord gave me Luke 6:38, and I read it to my kids.

> Give and you will receive. Your gift will return to you in full—pressed down, shaken

together to make room for more, running over, and poured into your lap. The amount you give will determine the amount you get back. (Luke 6:38)

Hallelujah, we praised God with all our hearts and the seed of faith was now being planted in our hearts.

- Why the Armor of God Is Important

Every day I would go across the street to the golf course before sunrise to walk around the course praying and praising God, and then I would sit near the bubbling brook enjoying the green grass and my quiet time with God, praying and reading His Word. My favorite scripture was Psalm 23, and I even memorized it and pray it every day since. As I was walking and praying, I stopped suddenly and looked down, and on the ground was a rusty black railroad spike about six inches long. I immediately picked it up, and God told me to keep this as a reminder of the spikes that nailed Him to the cross for me. He was crucified for the sins of the world, and I fell to my knees and cried and thanked God for showing that to me so now I could remember the cross and what He had done for me. It is amazing how I have used that spike while ministering in the nursing homes telling people Who Jesus is and what He has done for us and for this world.

I fell more in love with Jesus with every new day, praying and praising Him and loving Him with all my heart, soul, mind, and body. I wanted to read His Word daily so I can become like Jesus full of love, joy, peace, kindness, goodness, faithfulness and self-control. I wanted to tell the world about my Jesus because He is the Word, the Word was with God, and the Word is God. The Word became flesh and dwelt among us, and His name is Jesus Christ. The Word is the spirit of prophecy, and He lives in me, hallelujah. I wanted to fill myself with the Word because He is the truth and the life.

So I continue to ask Him, "Is there any offence hidden in my heart, Lord? Is there any rocky ground so your Word cannot take root? Hammer of the Word of God will break the rocky ground in my heart, so revive me, Lord, with your weed-whacker!"

I wanted so much to be cleansed and washed in His precious Blood so I can be transformed into His image and likeness.

He said, "Beware of intimidation, it's where the word *timid* comes from. That brings fear, doubt, unbelief, and selfishness, all of which I was being set free of." God says, "Whose report will you listen to, Satan or God's?"

Will you believe the doctor's evil report or God's Word that will bring life and health to your flesh? Faith comes by hearing and hearing the Word of God. Fear comes from hearing and hearing the words of Satan. I learned that whatever words I listened to would determine my destination. Words will set the course of your life. If you listen to Satan, he opens the door to fear, and you take the road to death. You will have more fear of death than when you got the bad report from the doctor. Fear is afraid of fear. Spirit of fear is afraid that you will not obey it and Satan will lose. You win when you rebuke fear and walk in faith. God wins, and Satan dies.

"So whose report will you believe," God asks, "Mine or the world's?"

I choose to believe God's Holy Word.

- God Is Teaching Me How to Fight Fear

I endured another challenge while walking in the golf course to pray, sing, and praise God one early morning before the golfers came out. A huge German shepherd dog not on a leash was running toward me, barking and looking like I could be his next meal. I thought at first it was a coyote, and I was beginning to fear. I started to pray for help and asked God what to do. He reminded me to call out to Jesus and use His name to rebuke the enemy who comes to steal, kill, and destroy me. I was still scared, but I kept shouting the name of Jesus, and the dog came right to me barking and growling. But the funny thing was, I saw his mouth barking, but I couldn't hear the noise. It was as if I was lifted up in the air, looking down on the dog, and as I spoke the name of Jesus, he would not attack me. After a few minutes, I heard his owner calling his name and running up to us. I could see how Jesus was teaching me how to defend myself by calling on His name because He is our refuge and our strength, and He is always there to help us when we call on him. The man apologized several times, and it gave me a few minutes to tell him about Jesus Christ and how He comes to my *rescue* always.

Not only was God teaching me to be strong in Him when the enemy attacks, but also to embrace His Word and trust Him with patience. He does not want me to walk by my feelings or the situations that challenge me but to believe His Word. When I speak it with authority, He comes to my *rescue*, and He assigns His angels to obey it and perform it when I speak it. So He allows these trials and temptations so I can learn from them by putting on the full armor of God daily!

Ephesians 6: The Armor of God

A final word: Be strong in the Lord and in his mighty power. Put on all of God's armor so that you will be able to stand firm against all strategies of the devil. For we are not fighting against flesh-and-blood enemies, but against evil rulers and authorities of the unseen world, against mighty powers in this dark world, and against evil spirits in the heavenly places.

Therefore, put on every piece of God's armor so you will be able to resist the enemy in the time of evil. Then after the battle, you will still be standing firm. Stand your ground, putting on the belt of truth and the body armor of God's righteousness. For shoes, put on the peace that comes from the Good News so that you will be fully prepared.

In addition to all of these hold up the shield of faith to stop the fiery arrows of the devil. Put on salvation as your helmet, and take the sword of the Spirit, which is the Word of God. Pray at all times and on every occasion. Stay alert and be persistent in your prayers for all believers everywhere.

- God Moments to Trust: He Kills the Termites

One day I was praying and interceding in my prayer room when I immediately felt the need to stop praying and to run down stairs for some unknown urgency. When I got there, the room was crawling with termites all over the walls, windows, and curtains. I began to call upon the name of Jesus and was cursing the termites as I called on Jesus. It was so amazing. I really could not believe my eyes as I watched the termites fall to the floor dead. I went to fetch my vacuum cleaner, and as they were falling to the floor dying, I vacuumed them up, and they were gone! It became another testimony of the power of God and speaking the mighty name of Jesus. Now I know why God had me journaling all my testimonies during my Christian walk with Him. He wanted me to write a book so that I could tell the world of His mighty power so that everyone would glorify His name.

- God Moments to Heal: He Saves the Fish

Another time I accidently killed my children's four gold fish. After I cleaned the fish tank, I filled it with warm water that obviously was not cold enough for the fish. That next morning when we all woke up, the fish were floating on top of the fish tank dead. We were shocked and very upset.

I said to them, "Let us kneel at the fish tank, join our faith in God, and pray for them."

As I lifted each fish out of the water, I prayed a pray of faith for their healing like God tells us in the Bible. So we did just that. We prayed for one fish at a time, and I gently put them back into the water. Before you knew it, the mouths of each fish began to move and breathe and swim into the tank. We were shouting for joy and praising God for this remarkable miracle. My kids had a testimony for school that week at "Show and Tell" as well as sharing their testimony to the church the following Sunday.

Let me tell you what *testimony* means so that you will understand why I must share these testimonies of God's miracles, or my "God moments."*

The Latin root for *testimony* is *testis*, meaning "witness." "Eye witness *testimony*" is a phrase you will also hear often in legal discussions. An object can also give testimony—without speaking, of course.

It seemed that the testimonies kept coming as God was teaching me how to put our faith into action and be patient to trust Him, to believe His Holy Word and to glorify Him. I told my kids that you need to go through the test in order to get a testimony. And God was giving us testimonies so that He could teach us how to obey Him.

> But Samuel replied, "What is more pleasing to the LORD: your burnt offerings and sacrifices or your obedience to his voice? Listen! Obedience is better than sacrifice, and submission is better than offering the fat of rams." (1 Samuel 15:22)

More Testimonies of God Teaching Me Obedience and Commitment

Here are more testimonies I want to share with you. I pray your patience will endure and that you enjoy the power of Jesus Christ and His mighty grace, forgiveness, and love.

I recall when I worked at a day care center and I was approached by another teacher. She told me that I needed to obey God and learn how to commit to Him. Being a new Christian at the time, I wondered why God told her and not me. Apparently I did not heed her words of advice and I divorced my husband rather than

---

* *Testimony* means "an assertion offering firsthand authentication of a fact."

obey God. I recall many years later that it took years for me to learn this lesson with many, many hardships, disappointments, pain, and suffering. It was the same play that I was a part of, but a different cast and a different stage. What I needed to learn was to love and accept myself and to love and obey God Who always knows what is best for me. That was a long and hard lesson to learn forty or so years later. I have so many testimonies to prove that God is in control of my life, that He loves me, forgives me, and disciplines me so I would learn to obey Him. I always ask myself, "Why can't God just come down and speak with me rather than let me suffer with my mistakes?" I guess when I see Him someday, I will be sure to ask Him. Why, oh, why is this life so difficult to become righteous and holy? I guess because He loves us that much, and He wants us to spend eternity with Him, Who is a holy and righteous God. He must transform us into His image and likeness because He cannot let sin and unrighteous live in His Holy presence in heaven.

> I will give you a new heart and put a new spirit in you; I will remove from you your heart of stone and give you a heart of flesh. (Ezekiel 36:26)

- Another Example of How I Learned Obedience

When I accepted Jesus Christ as my Lord and Savior I thought I knew it all. I would say to everyone that I did not need any insurance because I had the assurance of God in my life. Well, I took that to believe that I did not need home insurance, so I planned to cancel mine in Melrose where I lived. Being newly divorced, my husband was not a believer at the time, and he was overwhelmed and angry with me. So this was how God told me that I was wrong and that my ex-husband was correct; you do not cancel your home insurance. My cousin's wife had recently passed away, so I offered to take their daughter for the weekend of Mother's Day, hoping to bring her some comfort and peace. She was only about eight years old at the time, and she could spend some nice family time with my two children that were around the same age. We were all sitting in the living room watching a movie and eating popcorn when she got up from the couch to go to the bathroom. She stepped over our dog, a German shepherd, who was lying on the floor sleeping. The dog got so startled that he jumped up and somehow bit her in the face. It was so gross, so deep a cut on her face that we had to rush her to the hospital. She had many stitches on her cheek, and my cousin was so upset because the doctor said she could not have plastic surgery until after she was eighteen years old. As a result, I was sued for $250,000 to pay for her hospital expenses. My cousin's lack of forgiveness caused much dissension and heartbreak to our family. Then we had to put our dog down and that was extremely painful for my family.

The moral of the story—I learned to listen to my husband and obey God rather than sacrifice. That happened weeks before I was canceling the home insurance.

The rest of the story—I saw my cousin's daughter twenty years later as I was walking into McDonald's in Salem, Massachusetts. I went to the counter to order, and there she was. I immediately cried and asked her if she remembered me, and of course, she did. I repented to her with tears and a heart of compassion and told her how beautiful she was. She did have her plastic surgery, and she was a beautiful young lady. I shared my faith in Jesus with her, and she was so happy and blessed that we were a family again. Her father forgave me as well, and our family was reunited again, and we are good friends to this day.

- A Neighbor Gets a Word from God and Answers Our Prayers

Another week, while we were learning to trust God to meet our needs, we sat down to write a food shopping list to God.

We still hadn't received any alimony since our divorce case was not settled, so we had to trust God to meet our needs. This particular Friday, we sat and wrote our list, put it in an envelope, prayed together, and lifted it up to God. On Saturday night there was a knock on our door. When we answered the door, a woman introduced herself as our neighbor, and she said that while she was praying that morning, God spoke to her that a neighbor needed food and to go and food shop for them. We were shocked as she and her two children brought bags of shopping into the house. When the table was packed with bags, she prayed for God to richly bless us. Then she handed me a long-stemmed red rose and said it was from God. We thanked her, but I was crying. You see, red roses were my favorite flower, and I always wanted someone to bring me roses, and God did. We unloaded the grocery bags to find out that everything we had on our list was now on our table. Even to the name of the frozen pizza my kids loved. We share that testimony to show the faithfulness of God. And He is always on time.

- A Testimony of the Faithfulness of God

It was wintertime, and we still prayed to God to meet our needs every day. Usually, my kids got involved in prayer when we needed food for the week, and then they loved to pray to see what miracle God will do. Today it was snowing pretty hard, and we were homebound and wondering where our next miracle would come from. It was the end of the day, around 4:00 p.m., when two women, cold and wet from the snowfall, knocked on our door. One of the women asked if this was the house that was selling a fireplace mantle this past spring. I agreed, and she asked if it was still on sale. I said, "Well, it is sitting in the garage," and she asked if she could see it. We put on our coats, and they followed us to the garage. Yes, that was the one they wanted, and I told them they could take it; that gave me more room in the garage for my car. As they proceeded to take it and put it onto their shoulders, one lady took a $50 bill from her coat pocket and handed it to me. Hallelujah, we thanked them and rejoiced because now we had food money for the week.

And that is how my story continues for forty more years of serving my Lord and Savior, Jesus Christ, and His blessings keep on coming! I believe because Jesus was now the author and finisher of my faith. (Hebrew 12:2)

- Another God Moment While Sitting in Church

Another "God moment" happened while sitting in church one Sunday. When the pastor asked the congregation to turn to a scripture, which I proceeded to do so, I found a $20 bill. Then every time I turned to another scripture that he mentioned, another $20 bill showed up. By the end of the service, we had a total of $100. That's a miracle I will always remember of God's faithfulness. When I give it to God in a tithe, God always doubled the amount back in return. I have never been seen begging for bread or without, and it has been over forty years of tithing and God blessing us in return.

Once I was young, and now I am old. Yet
I have never seen the godly abandoned or their
children begging for bread. (Psalm 37:25)

Oh, how I get so excited sharing my "God moments" with you. I pray that encourages people and gives you faith to believe in a holy and awesome God. Can I keep sharing the wonders of my faithful God? My lobster story is one of my favorite stories to share…

- My Lobster Miracle from God

I finally get a "girls night out," and a miracle happened because of my obedience to God! I always celebrate my spiritual birthday on August 14 alone with my Lord every year. So this particular year, my girlfriends asked me to go to dinner with them, and I agreed to pick them up, and we were all going for dinner in Rockport to celebrate my blessed event. I was so excited to finally have a day off and to celebrate that special day with friends. Usually, I have spent August 14 alone with the Lord like I said. So this was my first time to go out with the girls, and I was a bit hesitant, and then I thought I had better ask the Lord first. It seemed okay since my kids' father was picking them up for a sleepover to Watertown where he lived since our divorce. So I was in the shower, and I asked Him if it was okay that I was going out with the girls.

I heard God emphatically say, "No, I want you to spend your birthday with Me," and to call and cancel the date with my girlfriends.

I resisted with, "Oh, no, Lord. I am looking forward to this dinner with the girls."

But God was adamant and said, "Cancel it, I need you to stay home with Me."

I began to cry uncontrollably and had to get out of the shower to cry and argue with my Father. I got angry with Him and said, "They are waiting for me to pick them up in one hour, Lord."

I realized then that you do not argue with God and you obey Him. "Trust and obey" became my motto.

So I called them, and they did not understand at all, but I just said, "I need to obey God, not man. I must cancel, and I am very sorry."

I dressed, put on a praise tape, and began singing praises to my Lord and dancing and praising Him. The more I praised, the more I loved Him, and my heart was filled with so much joy I could hardly contain it. In fact, I never thought of my friends again. The glory of the Lord filled my home with praise and thanksgiving, and the joy of the Lord became my strength like never before. I think I cried with joy and tears probably for two hours nonstop. I confessed to God that I don't live by bread alone but by every word that came from the mouth of God. Then I got my Bible, and I told God, "Let's feast on your Word tonight, Lord."

So as I was walking down the stairs to get my Bible, the doorbell rang. I immediately looked out the window, but there were no cars in sight. "Hmmm," I thought, "who rang the bell?"

I went and checked the back door, and when I opened it, there was a paper bag on the landing. I brought it in, and when I opened it, to my shock it was a live lobster and a huge baked potato. I cried hard tears and kept thanking God for this surprise. My father was providing a dinner for the two of us, and it was my favorite…lobster and baked potato. I set the table for two, prepared the food, and lit candles, and I had the best birthday celebration with my Heavenly Father. We praised and prayed and read the Word all night. Ever since that day, I have always spent August 14, my spiritual birthday, alone with my Lord and Savior Jesus Christ.

> The Lord your God is living among you
> Carol, He is your mighty savior. He will take
> delight in you with gladness. With His love,
> He will calm all your fears; He will rejoice
> over you with joyful songs! (Zephaniah 3:17)

Walking in blizzard   Nana is healed

- A Walk in the Blizzard as God Teaches Me to Hear His Voice

Another "God moment" to share with you was when God told me in prayer on this blistery-cold winter day to go and visit my Nana who lived in an apartment house in Malden, Massachusetts. It was a very bad winter blizzard, and I asked God, "What I should do?"

He told me to get a large heavy-duty shopping bag and fill it with a coffee pot, coffee, sugar and cream, and some muffins I had baked the day before. He told me to dress very warm because I was to take a walk and visit my Nana in Malden. Shocked and hesitant, I dressed, filled my shopping bag, and I started walking down the Parkway, and yes, I was bundled up for the inclement weather and probably looked foolish in man's eyes. I even began to feel foolish that God would ask me to do this, especially when there was no one on the road. The wind was howling, and the snow was freezing on my face. I fought hard to not doubt God, but deep in my heart, I believed He told me to do this. As I walked, I began to sing songs to the Lord, praising Him with all of my heart. When

I got to the high school, the wind began to howl even worse, and I became fearful that I couldn't actually make it to Malden. Then the Lord spoke to me and told me to speak to the wind and snow and command them to stop and to ask the sun to come out of the clouds and warm me up. He told me to do this in the name of His Son, Jesus Christ, and to believe. I obeyed and spoke the words He gave me, and I spoke the blood of Jesus on me and commanded the wind and snow to stop and for the sun to come out and warm me up. Within minutes, the wind ceased, the snow stopped falling. And the sun, as bright as a hot summer's day, came out and warmed me so much that within minutes, I had to remove my hat, scarf, and unbuttoned my jacket. There was now "a pep in my step," and I continued to walk, to sing and praise God all the way to her apartment house. But when I finally arrived and rang the doorbell, there was no answer. I got worried and asked God again what to do.

So I went to see the maintenance man, and I told him God instructed me to visit my Nana and she was not answering her door and I knew that she was home. I kindly asked him to unlock her door for me, which he did, and we found her passed out on the floor. I immediately knelt down and prayed for my Nana, asking God to heal her in Jesus's name. I remembered reading the day before about Elisha praying over a child that had died, and he breathed on her the breath of life, and she came back to life. So I prayed that prayer over my Nana and breathed on her, and she suddenly opened her eyes and sat up and was so happy to see me. We helped her get back into her bed, and I encouraged him to leave as she was fine and I would spend the day with her. I put on a pot of coffee that I brought, and then around noontime, her two daughters showed up on their lunch hour, and they too were so surprised to see me. I told them what transpired and how God put Nana on my heart to come and visit with her and how I found her on the floor and how God told me to pray for her. We all prayed together in thanksgiving, and my two aunts, who were my dad's twin sisters, and my nana, accepted Jesus Christ as their Lord and Savior that day. We all praised God as we enjoyed each other and our coffee and muffins! Many years have passed, but I still thank God that all three of them are in heaven and one day we will meet again. I am so blessed and full of thanksgiving to my Lord, Who always leads and guides me in His perfect will. This is when I stopped relying on myself and I learned to rely on God who even raises the dead. Hallelujah (2 Corinthians 1:8-9)

- God's Perfect Timing as We Hear God's Voice and Obey

I need to share this amazing "God moment" when I and my prayer partner and best friend were praying and interceding for our community and God gave us an assignment to take a walk around our neighborhood. As we were walking around the streets and praying, an ambulance pulled up to a house right in front of us. The EMTs rushed into the house with a stretcher, and we were asking God what He wanted us to do. He told us to enter the house as well and pray for whoever needed prayer. We obeyed, and an elderly lady was on the stretcher unconscious. We prayed in the Holy Spirit, and then we told the EMTs that God wanted us to pray for her anointing her with healing oil. She immediately opened her eyes, and she began to praise God. They were all giving God the honor due Him, but they still had to take her to the hospital to be checked. However, they thanked us on the way out. We did visit her later that week, and she was fine and very thankful to God for leading us to her home at that perfect time. God was doing so many remarkable things in our lives as we continued to get together every morning and pray to God for His people. God speaks to us in His Holy Bible and directs us where to go and for whom to pray.

Oh, the joys of those who are kind to
the poor and needy! The Lord rescues them

when they are in trouble. The LORD protects
them and keeps them alive. (Psalm 41:1–3)

• God Answers My Prayers

God is blessing me every day and answering my prayers as well.
Every day I would take a walk either in the neighborhood, the golf
course across the street (not during golfing hours), or I would go to
Nahant Beach. I would go to the beach even in the cold winter days
dressed in my long down coat, boots, hat, and gloves—it did not
matter! I just love the ocean and the calmness and peace it offers me.

One day in midafternoon, I was walking briskly along the
ocean when I realized my blood sugar was dropping. I began to
sweat, and then I remembered that I forgot to put some fruit
or candy in my pocket. Panic hit me as I cried out to God for
help. I could not take another step as I was getting weaker by
the second; there were no people in sight or a store in the area,
nor did I have any energy to go any further.

"Lord, what do I do now?" I cried. "Forgive me for forgetting, Lord, please help me!"

Suddenly, I looked down on the sand, and I saw a couple
pieces of wrapped hard candy, and I was so shocked that God
would put them in front of me, as if they dropped out of the
heavens. So I blessed them, offered them to God, removed the
paper wrapping, and ate them.

These are the instances that God puts in my life to build
my faith and to truly know that He is alive and well and always
hears my cry for help. He said in Isaiah 59:1,

> Behold, the LORD's hand is not so short
> that it cannot save; nor is His ear so dull that
> it cannot hear.

Hallelujah!

I just love to tell of all God's mercies and of His love. I can just talk about the Lord and His wonderful works to all His children. That is why I believe it is important to journal every day, because then you can share God's miracles and moments to those He puts in your path. Perhaps they too will believe in Jesus, and that is why sharing your testimonies is so very important!

> But the time is coming—indeed it's here now—when true worshipers will worship the Father in spirit and in truth. The Father is looking for those who will worship him that way. (John 4:23)

- God Is Always with Me

It was in August, while I was driving to my destination on Route 128 and praying in the Holy Spirit for about thirty minutes, and suddenly, the traffic came to sudden halt. As I looked in my rearview mirror, I saw vehicles coming to a screeching halt and thought instantly that they would crash into me from behind. There was no time to think, so in that exact moment, I called on the name of Jesus. A trailer truck stopped next to me, and with his loud horn, he directed me to quickly move in front of him to avoid the upcoming deadly crash! I cannot describe this miraculous scene except it was real and God protected me that moment. God said in His Word that He would give us His mighty angels to protect us and they would obey His Word when we speak it to our adversaries! Even the people who came out of their cars to discuss this sudden-to-be accident said they definitely saw a miracle from God! So I thank You, God, for Your divine protection and Your amazing love and faithfulness.

> Then I called on the name of the LORD:
> "Please, LORD, save me!" How kind the LORD

is! How good he is! So merciful, this God of ours! The LORD protects those of childlike faith; I was facing death, and he saved me. Let my soul be at rest again, for the LORD has been good to me. He has saved me from death, my eyes from tears, my feet from stumbling. (Psalm 116:4–8)

- Another God Moment: When He Finds My Missing Key

I was walking along Nahant Beach for about six miles, singing and praising God, when exhaustion hit me and I decided I'd better head back to my car. It was such a brisk and windy day, but the sun was bright, the sky was so blue, and that was keeping me warm. I headed to my car as I got to the end of the beach and bent down to get my car key, which I tied to the shoelace of my sneaker. To my dismay and shock, there was no key. Of course, I was frightened and horrified. "Oh, Lord," I cried, "now what, where is my key?" I told my Lord that I needed Him now more than ever. Since He always hears my cry for help and answers my prayers, I cried again, "Lord, help me!"

I began to walk back on the beach to follow my steps and wait for God to stop me when He saw my key—at least that was what I asked Him to do. "Lord, I trust You now as always, and please don't disappoint me," I cried. So I walked back on the beach, and would you believe that, about four miles down the beach I heard God say, "Stop." I obeyed His small, still voice, looked down on the sand, and there was my key. The wind did not even cover the key with the sand, but there it was lying on top of the sand. I knelt down, wept in thanksgiving, and that was how God continued to teach me to trust Him. The trials and sufferings in my life always bring me to my knees because He always blesses me and teaches me to trust Him and not lean on my own understanding but in all ways acknowledge Him, and He will make a straight path for my life.

> But in my distress I cried out to the LORD;
> yes, I prayed to my God for help. He heard me
> from his sanctuary; my cry to him reached his
> ears. (Psalm 18:6)

• Another God Moment When He Finds My Eyeglasses

Another journal entry took place at the beach while on my six-mile walk this warm and windy day. I began to get tired and realized I had another six miles to get back to my car. I made it back to the car and headed home. But when I got there, I began searching for my glasses and panicked because they weren't on the top of my head as I had thought. I cried out to my Father, "Where did I leave my glasses, Lord?" You see, I talk with the Lord like that because He is the friend and lover of my soul, and He always hears me and answers me. So He reminded me that I left them on the blanket at the beach before I took the walk.

"But I thought they were on my head," I told Him. "I shook the blanket," I said, "and it is a windy day, so they must be hidden in the sand by now. Oh no, now what do I do? I will not remember where I was sitting nor will I find them in the sand." I panicked!

"Have no fear," He reminded me to trust Him always!

So, reluctantly, I resolved to go back to the beach and let Him show me where they are. As crazy as this sounds, I parked where I thought I was parked and began walking down the beach. The wind was so bad that I began to feel foolish as now the beach was empty as it was getting pretty late. But I persisted and kept walking until I felt like He told me to stop. I knelt and felt the sand, and there were my red reading glasses under the sand. Let me tell you how I cried with thanksgiving to my faithful God. He never lets me down and He fills me with such joy and thanksgiving that I cannot even contain it. Since then, I have gained some wisdom and have accumulated many pairs of eyeglasses. God fills me with joy and laughter, which humbles me to no end!

Because God bends down to listen, I will
pray as long as I have breath! (Psalm 116:2)

- The Beginning of God's Calling to Go and Tell

I believe God is calling me to make a more serious commitment to visit hospitals and nursing homes. I think because I visited my grandma in the hospital every week, I felt called to visit other patients in her ward. When I did, they would open their hearts to me and let me pray with them. Sometimes I would go to the music room down the hall and just sing praise songs to the Lord.

Many were drawn to Him in me, and before I realized it, wheelchairs would come by and listen to me singing, and then I would pray for them. That is when I believe God was putting the nursing home ministry on my heart. I started to go from room to room to those who were bedridden and pray with them.

I met one lady who just laid in her bed depressed and angry, and every time I visited her, she wanted me to leave. One day, I asked her if I could just sing to her and maybe that would help her to feel better. Her legs were amputated, and my heart just wept for her. That day when she listened to my song, which was "Jesus Loves You," she could not stop crying and told me that her grandmother sang that song to her when she was a child.

By the next week, she allowed me to clean her up, comb her hair, and push her around the hospital and even take her outdoors for fresh air. She said she hadn't smelled fresh air or felt the warm breeze on her face in years and she was enjoying her life again.

She now looked forward to my weekly visits with joy; and I looked forward to see God bless her and save her soul.

There is no greater joy than to see a child of God repent of their sins and accept Jesus Christ into their heart to be their Lord and Savior.

• More Encouragement by God to Go and Tell

I am working full-time at a law firm in Boston and visiting hospitals and nursing homes part-time. Then suddenly I was faced with sickness that I never expected to happen to me.

I was commuting by train daily, and various symptoms began to attack my body. I would run to catch a train only to realize that I forgot my purse at the office and had to go back to the office and then miss the train. Some days, I would get on the train and be so exhausted that I would fall asleep only to wake up in the wrong city in a panic. I would need to wait for another train to return home in the darkness of the night.

Another symptom was the need to eat something sweet every day, and I began to hide candy bars everywhere. I would be extremely thirsty, needing water and felt that I would die without it.

Then I noticed that I was eating hot fudge sundaes and chocolate bars after lunch, but I wasn't gaining weight but losing weight. At first, I was happy to lose weight and not have to go on another fad diet. When people commented on my weight loss, I would say I was "thinking thin," and it was working.

I began to fall asleep at my desk every day after lunch, and my boss became more concerned; he was worried and encouraged me to call my doctor. I was stubborn, and I did not take his advice until I passed out on my way to work one morning.

I was taken to a local hospital and then transferred to Joslin Diabetes Center in Boston, where I was diagnosed and treated for type one diabetes; I was immediately put on insulin.

I gained weight within days, and the need for sugar subsided, but I was always thirsty, and water became a necessity.

Before that hospital experience and diagnosis, I had been training for the Boston marathon and jogging up to twenty miles a few times a week. I contributed the weight loss to my daily exercise routine.

I was then disqualified from the Boston marathon and became disappointed and depressed with my prognosis. I recall Bill Rogers, ministering to me with encouragement, said that one day, I would run the race again, which I never did.

Meeting Bill Rogers encouraging me to never quit the race…

But God was not done with me. I began to run another race for Christ, who began to use me in a mighty way ministering to the patients at Joslin and encouraging them with God's love and redemptive power.

I recall ministering to a Jewish woman and her husband who wanted so much to know my Jesus, and soon they accepted Jesus Christ as their Lord and Savior.

About a month later, when I was released from Joslin, I got a call from her husband thanking me for sharing Jesus with them. He told me that his wife had gone home to Jesus and was no longer suffering and that he longed to see her one day in heaven.

That is when God began to lead me to go and tell the good news to all those who would listen to His mighty call for redemption and salvation. I accepted God's call to the ministry of intercessory prayer and evangelism in hospitals and nursing homes with a humble and joyful heart.

Now all glory to God who is able, through His mighty power at work within us, to accomplish infinitely more than we might ask or think. Hallelujah!

• A Great Hospital Testimony of Mary

Another great testimony happened when I would go to the hospital in Cambridge to visit my grandma. I would take my mother with me so she could stay with her mother all day. I would visit other patients as well, and God always showed me which room to visit. The doctor in charge was not happy with me visiting there because I would get the patients happy when I sang songs to them in the music room, and some shouted for joy and raised their hands to heaven. What a joy that was for me to witness. Tons of wheelchairs would follow me around, singing and praising God. Some days the director would escort me out the door, and I would enter into the hospital from another entrance and go to another floor. One day he asked me why I kept coming back when he told me not to. I simply told him that God told me to, and I must obey God, not man. He would get so aggravated with me and send me away. That just made me more tenacious and strong in the Lord! I would go in the parking lot and bind the enemy with the power and authority of Jesus Christ.

There was a woman named Mary that the Lord had me visit every week. I would go into her room, even though she was in a coma for months, and I would sit by her bed and read the book of Psalms to her. Then I would pray over her and say, "Goodbye, until the next week." The nurses told me to stop coming because she couldn't even hear me, but I said, "I obey God, not man, and He told me to come and pray with her, so I obey God."

One Friday afternoon, God's miracle came true. When I was done praying and was about to leave her room, she sat up in her bed and cried in a loud voice, "Thank you, Carol, I love you, and I love JESUS!" I ran to her, and when I did, she smiled at me, and then she lay down and closed her eyes. She went to heaven that moment, and the nurse witnessed the entire miracle. I cried and thanked God with all my heart and soul. That story still makes me cry when I remember that blessed day.

> All who calls upon the Name of the Lord
> will be saved. (Romans 10:13)

Yes I was confident I would see the Lord's goodness while I am here in the land of the living. I waited patiently for the Lord, I was brave and courageous and yes, I waited patiently for my Lord and He did not disappoint me. Thank you Jesus. (Psalm 27:13-14)

• God's Ministry Begins in Hospitals and Nursing Homes

My grandma that was in a hospital because she broke her hip was now being transferred to a nursing home for physical therapy. That was a sad time for us because my grandma was a strong and healthy woman who worked hard all of her life caring for her family and running a seamstress business in her basement. She is the one who made the gown for the Blessed Mother statute at the Vatican in Italy. When the hospital had done all that they could for her, she was sent to a nursing facility in Revere, Massachusetts. That was a very unpleasant memory for me as well as a horrific ending to her life. This was the facility that abused my grandmother, and when we found out, we reported those incidents, and the facility was shut down, and legal ramifications were now in progress. I decided then as an advocate for my family that I would get the justice that my grandma deserved. I believe it is imperative to hold those who might be responsible for these atrocities accountable by pursuing legal action, which we did. It is imperative to prevent such atrocities to continue in these facilities. That particular facility in Revere was shut down, and justice was taken.

My grandmother died during this process; it was the beginning of my prayer and intercession for nursing home staff, the residents, and their families. I truly believe God is calling me to initiate a nursing home ministry at my church; I pray God's will to be done in my life.

> For God so loved the world that whosoever believes in Him shall not perish but have eternal life. (John 3:16)

Grandma dies in nursing home

Chapter 5

Salem

My Cousin Patty

I began another chapter in my life as a single woman after my divorce, and I moved to Salem, which is a city north of Boston.

It was then that my children had graduated from college. My son started his own business and lived in Arlington while my daughter moved to Atlanta, Georgia to begin her career. I was now alone from the ones I truly loved and missed. We suffered a church split and everyone went their own way. I missed the love and fellowship that I was accustomed to from my children, my church, and my Christian brothers and sisters.

Salem is famous for its witch trials in 1692, where locals were executed for practicing witchcraft. I am not fond of witchcraft, but I chose to live there to be close to my cousin who found me an available apartment across the street from hers. I believed it was a safe choice for me at that time in my life.

I secured a great job at a local law firm, and I was able to walk to work every day. I loved being near the ocean; I enjoyed walking through the town to the laundromat, food shopping, restaurants; and I felt safe to jog every evening after work around the common because it was fully lit.

My cousin worked in a local restaurant on the water, and we dined together some nights during her dinner break. I rode my bike all over the North Shore on weekends. This seemed to be the best time of my life.

However, I later learned that October was a tough month to live in Salem with the traffic and the witchcraft that permeated the town of Salem. Nor was I aware that witches would inhabit the second floor of the house in which I lived. That was challenging as you will read later in my book.

One Friday, while working at the law firm and anticipating a restful weekend ahead, the secretary of my physician's office called me with the results of my routine mammogram. Very coldly, she said that I had a malignant tumor on my left breast. I was shocked, fearful, and angry and asked why she and not my doctor would call me to schedule an appointment to personally share that dreadful news. I spent the entire sleepless weekend in fear and trepidation.

On Monday morning, I went to the office to meet with my doctor to discuss the diagnosis and prognosis. Now my doctor, fully aware that I had a diabetic condition, let me sit in the waiting room from 9:00 a.m. until 5:00 p.m. with no acknowledgment of my presence; she simply left the office for the day. I was furious, hurt, and disappointed.

When I discussed this with my attorney, she suggested that I schedule three appointments with various surgeons to biopsy my breast. I made the appointments, and a few weeks later all three biopsies were negative for cancer. Of course, I was thrilled and excited.

I thanked God for another miracle in my life. However, I was angry with the doctor who had her secretary call me that Friday with the horrific news of malignant cancer. After my attorney pursued the doctor for an explanation, her only defense was that she read the wrong report. I never received a telephone call or letter of apology from her.

I had another opportunity to forgive, but I found a new primary care physician.

God was teaching me to trust Him and not man. God is my Lord and Savior and my great and mighty physician who has never let me down. I must always be aware that there is an enemy—the devil and/or Satan—who is out to kill, steal, and destroy God's children. You will read more of how the devil has tried to destroy me and my faith in God. (See John 10:10.)

- God's Training Me to Hear His Voice and Obey

Bike-riding became my peace and solitude because I could pray on my long rides, and it seemed God would speak to me as I prayed in the Holy Spirit. On one particular day, God told me to get a half dozen submarine sandwiches and cans of soda and put them in my bike basket and head to Nahant Beach. I loved to hear God's voice when he told me to bless people. I rode all along the beaches from Salem to Swampscott and on to Nahant. When I saw a street person in need, God would have me stop and give them a lunch bag with a sub sandwich, a cold drink, and a small dessert. I just loved telling them it was from Jesus, Who loved them so much. I gave them the true story of Who Jesus was and what He did for them. I loved praying with them to invite Jesus into their heart. But one thing I noticed though—no one just opened the bag to eat. They just caressed the bag of food like it was gold. They held on to it so tightly and then put it in their wagon with their belongings. They enjoyed me telling them the story of Jesus more than the lunch, especially the part that Jesus loved them so much that He would bring them lunch. I've never seen anyone stop and eat their gift of food, but they really enjoyed eating of the bread of life from the Lord.

> People do not live by bread alone, but by every word that comes from the mouth of God. (Matthew 4:4)

- More of Gods Training to Hear His Voice and Obey

Another day when I was heading out to Nahant, God stopped me and said, "No...go to visit your mother." I was sad and almost began to argue with God, and I stopped my bike and told God I was sorry because I learned to never argue with God and to just trust Him and obey Him. I reversed my direction to head to my Mother's house in Peabody. God was teaching me to hear His voice and obey it. Even though I did not know why He was telling me to go, I obeyed. When I got to her house, there was a car parked in front, and it was my aunt and uncle, who were visiting my mom. So now I understood who I was praying for while I was riding my bike to Peabody—my aunt and uncle. My aunt complained about how awful she had been feeling, so I asked her if I could tell her about Jesus Christ and His miracle working power and because He loved her more than she could imagine. She was quite upset at her health condition and only continued to complain and murmur with her foul language! When I asked again if I could pray for her and to ask God to heal her, she refused. But my uncle immediately said yes.

"Can you pray for me?" he asked.

As we prayed together, my uncle accepted Jesus Christ to be his Lord and Savior. Then he felt so great that he begged my aunt to pray as well. It took him a few minutes to convince her to pray with me, but she finally did, and we were all praising Jesus Christ for His miracle working power of salvation. My mom served coffee and cake, and we all rejoiced for this miracle.

The following week, my uncle, who was the healthy one in his family, had a severe heart attack and suddenly died. My family grieved so much, but especially his wife, my aunt. I encouraged the family that my uncle was resting in the arms of Jesus in heaven. That really didn't help this sad family. The worst happened the following week… my aunt suffered a heart attack at her workplace and died. The workers found her flat on her face at her desk. A grief-stricken family losing both parents so fast was a heartfelt story. But for me, I was in awe of how God spoke to me to obey Him and go to my mother's house that day and not to the beach! Today both my aunt and uncle are in heaven together because of God's perfect timing and because God's ways are not our ways, and He is far greater than all man could ever think or imagine. And I am thankful that I obeyed Him! That was the greatest gift of all. They are in heaven, and someday I will see my family again.

• God Speaks to Me through a Pain in My Chest

While heading home on my bike and praying in the Spirit, I suddenly had a pain in my right breast chest area, and I was anxious to ask God why. When I got home and began to pray, my prayer partner called with news that her grandson was rushed to the hospital with a pain and lump on his right breast. She asked me to join her in prayer so we prayed, trusting God for His healing. Then around eleven thirty that evening, she called me again to tell me that the doctor just called and told her that her grandson was fine and there was no longer a lump on his breast. We wept in thanksgiving and praised God for healing her grandson.

Hallelujah forevermore! An amazing day that was, and these are the memories I treasure the most! I believe God hand tailored our blessings which He designed for our growth and benefit.

Isaiah 55:8 "For my thoughts are not your thoughts, neither are my ways your ways" declares the Lord."

- God Continues to Tell Me to Put On the Armor of God

One cold and snowy day, I felt impressed to make chicken soup and bake some bread and bring them across the street to visit my cousin. I put my package together, put on my boots and heavy coat, and walked outside. My house was on the corner of a busy street, so I was careful to look both ways before crossing the street to my cousin's house. Just as it was safe, I took a step off of the curb, but to my surprise, by boots stuck together, and I fell flat on my face, and the large Tupperware container hit my chest cavity so that I actually lost my breath. The bottle of soda water rolled down the street, and I lay there unable to breathe. I was so thankful that no cars were coming down the street at that time. When I was able to get up and retrieve the bottle, I continued to cross the street. When I made it to the sidewalk, my boots stuck together again, like the shoelace from the left boot stuck to the hook of the right boot. It was the strangest thing that I've ever seen. I proceeded to walk up the stairs to my cousin's house when the witch in her house on the second floor opened the door to say, "Well, that was quite a fall, you had better check your knee, it is bleeding pretty bad!" When I got upstairs I was surprised to see that my knee was pretty bad. That is why I despised living in a house with witches, and that is why God was teaching me to put on the full armor of God as in Ephesians 6!

It always seemed that whenever I obeyed God and did something great for Him, the devil always attacked me or try to rob me of my blessing. I was not only learning how to hear and obey

God, I was also learning every day how to fight the devil by putting on the armor of God as written in Ephesians 6. I also learned the importance of pleading the blood of Jesus on myself and my family, my home, and my life in Christ Jesus. It was a daily battle for sure. The battle continued when I got laid off from my job, and without rent, they were going to evict me from my apartment. In a way, I was not sad about the apartment because the witches lived on the second floor, and that was always a challenge for me seeing witches go in and out every day and night. I would hear animals screaming at night, and I never could sleep without praying for hours and pulling down the devil's strongholds!

> But the Lord stands beside me like a great warrior and before Him my persecutors will stumble. They cannot defeat me! (Jeremiah 20:11A)

I called my friend Donna to come over and pray with me so we could ask God for wisdom if I got evicted. I even called my mother to ask her if I could move in with her until I found another job, but she refused. I was feeling more rejection from my mother so I truly needed to hear from God. My dear friend was always trying to convince me to call her chiropractor because she thought if I started dating again, that would help me take my mind off my problems. But what I truly needed was wisdom from my Lord! Lord, I need to know what is your will for my life at this time?

• I Finally Decide to Call My Old Friend

After months of convincing me to call him, I finally asked her his name. When she said his name, I almost fell off the chair in shock. He and I dated in our high school days before he went to chiropractic school in Iowa. We both worked in a men's clothing store at the North Shore Mall when we were sixteen years old. I worked in the office, and Len was a salesman. I called his office and left a quirky message on his phone:

"If you are single and remember me, you can call me back, but if not, please disregard this call."

Within minutes he returned my call. He told me he always loved me, and yes, he would love to see me again. He arrived at my apartment within fifteen minutes. I was shocked when I answered the door because I expected a tall, thin kid as I remembered him, but I was so amazed at how tall and handsome he was. We walked around Salem and got to know each other again. We were both divorced with two children, so we decided to hang around and just be friends. I told him I was a born-again Christian and I didn't date non-Christians, and he didn't want to date a Christian either. That was fine with me, so we just got together and rekindled our friendship.

We visited my family, who remembered him from our high school years, and we all got along so well. Even my children liked him, and they too were hoping I would get married again. They hated seeing me always alone and hated to worry about me. After about three months, he asked my mother for my hand in marriage, and we got engaged. The weird thing was that he put a ring on my finger, and it was the exact ring I used to draw when I was a little girl. I used to trace my hand and put a three-diamond ring on my ring finger. The ring he gave me had three diamonds in a row, just like my drawings. We were married in May, and my kids stood up for me. His best friend stood up for him. It was a small wedding at the Ferncroft Hotel with only our immediate family in attendance. His daughters rejected me immediately as well as their mother. Unfortunately she knew we were an item forty years ago and that we loved each other back then. I was the last person she wanted her ex-husband to remarry. I believe now that we were anxious to get married and we did not consider his children and their feelings. The rejection just caused more suffering and pain. God said, "Do not be anxious about anything, but in every situation, by prayer and petition, with thanksgiving, present your requests to God" (Philippians 4:6). And be still and wait on God, which we did not do.

Not only were we anxious, but I also did not obey God because he really was not a Christian and I fell for that lie. I realized that I ignored 2 Corinthians 6:14 also… God said, "Do not marry a non-Christian for what does light have to do with darkness." That was my mistake. Not only did his children reject me, but even his dog had a difficult time with me. If I entered a room, she would leave that room. She went in and out of the house constantly using the dog door to avoid my presence. That was such a sad situation to see a dog so unhappy. I was so tempted to run away myself and let the dog have her master to herself!

It seemed that I always learned my lessons the hard way.

Thank God for the gift of repentance, and we thank God for His patience while we continue to grow in Him. Yes, we are grateful that God turns all things around for good to those who love Him (Romans 8:28). The good news is that his daughters eventually accepted Jesus Christ as their Lord and Savior after many years of prayer and thanksgiving. We have since become a loving family in Jesus Christ; and God has been highly favored, praised, and glorified.

We marry in 1996 with our immediate families

Chapter 6

Danvers

It was challenging to be married to a man whose children and their mother, as well as his dog, rejected me. She always knew that we dated years ago, and me marrying her ex-husband was just too difficult for her to deal with. Every day I prayed for my husband and his family with no sign of peace and reconciliation in sight. It was painful to have to suffer rejection day in and day out. And even the dog would not stay in the same room if I was there. I think both me and the dog were unhappy. We had a lovely catered party the following month in our back yard with our family and friends to celebrate our wedding. My kids and family loved Len, and I think it was because we all knew each other during our high school years, and we all got along so well back then.

Our marriage was difficult in the beginning, as mixed families need time to adjust, forgive, and love one another. Fishing, golfing, and hunting were his top priorities, and I soon took up golfing because he gave me a golf membership as a wedding gift at the Ferncroft Golf Club, and that brought some life and joy into my life. I golfed with a good friend after work, and I began to enjoy the sport. Len sponsored several golf tournaments at his chiropractic office, and that was a new experience for me as well. Len and his buddy owned a boat. We loved boating and fishing, and I was beginning to enjoy my new life. We traveled to islands, we dined in fine restaurants, and all that seemed new and adventurous for me. Now it was time for me to look for a full-time job.

Boating   Golfing

Fishing

- God Called Me on a Mission, and I Knew Not Why

I was searching for a full-time job now that I was married and living in Danvers. So much stress and time involved to interview the interviewer. I diligently worked day and night preparing for this new journey in my life. After this tedious search, I decided on a one-year contract at a job in a law firm in Saugus, Massachusetts. I signed the contract to fill in for an office manager, who was taking a medical leave to deal with a cancer diagnosis. I did not realize that this was a mission from God until the fight began. I became intimately involved in Ms. D's life as she trained me, and then she began her treatments. The weaker she became, the less she was able to come to work. That meant more work for me because God told me to visit her in the hospital, and that was when I realized it was a mission from God. She constantly needed intercessory prayer, love, encouragement, hope, faith, and salvation. There were surgeries to overcome and to heal from and a Legal Firm to deal with was very difficult. I think it was the worst persecution I have ever had to overcome, the most humiliating circumstances, and some of the most hateful and evil people to forgive and love. I thank God that I could overcome by the blood of the Lamb and the word of my testimony. I realized that I was called not only to overcome the persecution but to bring Ms. D. through her trials and tribulations by introducing her to Jesus Christ. She got to know Jesus Christ for the first time in her life and to trust Him, love Him, and hold His hand when times got too difficult for her. The cancer had spread throughout her body and she was now close to death. She then called for me from the ICU to pray and escort her home to our Lord in heaven. It was a bittersweet time for us to say farewell and with tears and love she went home in peace. No other family members were present. I was thankful that I obeyed God and accepted that job and overcame the persecution. I thank God that I was there for her to the very end when she left this earth and entered into eternity with God carrying her in His loving arms. The day she went home was the final day of my contract. How crazy was that. I learned the greatest lesson of all… Obedience is better than sacrifice. I obeyed God when I wanted to quit so many times, and I became stronger in Him and was able to stand still and know that He is my God. Most of all, I will love and remember Ms. D, and one day I will spend eternity with her forever. The journey ended and I was able to love and forgive those people at the law firm, and pray for my next assignment from God.

I began again to pray and look for a full-time job to help with the bills and our lifestyle. I did a lot of bike-riding and golfing on my time off, and I thought life was pretty good. I then found a great job as the assistant to the vice president of a large company in the North Shore, and I earned a great salary with six weeks' paid vacation time. However, I did need to deal with the stress of an arrogant president of the company who constantly abused me emotionally with his fowl mouth and his anger toward me. I always wanted to quit, but I used the challenges to learn to forgive the ugly and be patient that God would deliver me.

> For our struggle is not against flesh and blood, but against the rulers, against the authorities, against the powers of this dark world and against the spiritual forces of evil in the heavenly realms. (Ephesians 6:12)

I learned by now that I cannot quit a job but that God has me there for a reason and I will be patient and wait for Him to lead and guide me in His perfect will. Many people gave their life to Jesus at this job, and I was able to minister to the sick, the lost, the brokenhearted, and to all the people that God brought my way.

- Testimony of Answered Prayer When God Saved My Son on 9/11

It was my son's second wedding anniversary, and he had to fly to California for business the next morning. That night I called him to pray for him before he departed on the 8:45 a.m. flight, which he so often did on Monday mornings. I had my usual prayer time that day, and now while dressing for work in Beverly, my husband and his buddy shouted to me to come and watch the news of flight 93 crashing into the World Trade Center. I ran into the living room to see what was happening and remembered that my son was to be on that flight heading to California. I immediately fell to the floor as if someone knocked the wind out of me, screaming and crying that my son was on that flight. The pain in my heart was horrific, and I could not stop crying and screaming. My husband was trying to comfort me and was telling me to find out for sure. When I finally got some composure minutes later, I called my daughter-in-law to confirm the truth for me. She said that he was *not* on that flight because after he prayed last night, he decided to take the shut-eye flight at 1:00 a.m. rather than the 8:45 a.m. flight. I was so relieved, but I was still so upset that over three thousand people were killed by this horrific terrorist attack. I needed the strength to give praise and thanksgiving to God for sparing my son, but I needed to grieve the three thousand people that did not. I needed to pull myself together and still go to work and pray for those more unfortunate than myself. There were fellow employees who had family and friends either on that plane or working in the towers. I remember I had to give a presentation at 11:00 a.m., and when I got to work, I couldn't even think of my speech because I was so distraught. I went into the conference room and tried to pull myself together, but when I stood up to speak, I began to sing "God Bless America," and in minutes the entire room stood and joined me in singing. There was not a dry eye in the conference room. 9/11 is the day we will all remember as the deadliest day in history for the United States firefighters and responders. We will forever shed a tear for our country and for the lives that were lost.

> Give thanks to the Lord for He is good;
> His love endures forever. (Psalm 118:1)

- Testimony When God Heals My Knee and Then My Mother

One day while I was babysitting for my grandson, I fell off the playground slide and landed on both knees on a cement slab. I saw an orthopedic surgeon and was diagnosed with a torn meniscus of my knee, and I needed surgery. When I was at the doctor's office, my knee was so swollen and in pain.

As he examined me, he said, "Do you realize that there is no blood that flows into your knees? You really need surgery."

My reply shocked him when I said, "I had not realized that, but what I do know is that the blood of Jesus Christ flows through my body and will flow to my knee when I ask the Lord in prayer."

I then put my hands on my knee and asked the Lord to let His blood flow into my knee and bring me healing. The doctor chuckled, and as he did, the swelling left my knee, and it was completely healed right before his eyes. I walked out of his office in victory. I rode my bike over twenty miles that afternoon, praising God for my healing!

The funny thing is that the doctor remembered me and that testimony when years later I took my mother to see him for her back pain, and he said, "Aren't you the lady whose knee God healed in my office?"

I replied, "I sure am."

He said to my mother, "Maybe you should have your daughter pray for you so her Jesus will heal you as well."

She did get healed at the *Easter Pageant* at my church weeks later. We were walking out of the play right behind the cast member Mark, who played "Jesus," and she said, "If only I can touch the hem of His garment, I know I could be healed." The actor, "Jesus," turned around and asked her if she was following him, and he said to her, "Don't follow me but follow the real Jesus."

My mother did accept Jesus Christ as her Lord and Savior that night, and she was healed. She was off all her medications, including morphine due to the excessive pain in her body. She lived till she was almost ninety-one years young.

- A God Moment with My Mother in December

I woke up today depressed and with a negative attitude, which was very unusual for me. It was such a lovely day, but I was caring for my mother, and therefore, I was very tired and exhausted. She was aging and not feeling well, and she did not want to give up her house, her independence, nor did she ever want to go to a nursing facility. She begged me to care for her and not let that happen. I agreed not to ever put her in one. I quit my full-time job in Beverly making that bountiful salary, and God told me to care for my mother. That would be my next assignment. At first I told Him I did not want that job and realized I still held some bitterness in my heart toward her and God wanted to deliver me of that. So I quit and took on that responsibility to care for her. The company was gracious to me, gave me a severance, and I was able to train someone and left in peace. But there were days I complained and murmured, and this was one of them. My siblings were not living in Massachusetts, and therefore they were unable to bear the burden with me. That particular day, I went to Nahant Beach, my place of respite and peace with the Lord. I walked in the sixty-degree day, letting His sunshine warm my heart and open my ears that I might hear Him speak to me in my aloneness and distress. He reminded me when He said, "How can you say you love God when you cannot love those around you?"

"So I must die to myself, Lord, and love and forgive as Jesus did," I said.

Murmuring and complaining is sin, so I confessed my sins and did my cleansing of tears as He restored me and revived me once again. It was time now for me to care for my mother 24-7, and that responsibility became the greatest gift from God. I grew to love her, honor her, care for her, and best of all, bring her to Jesus Christ. You will read more of the blessed times in our life.

As I was driving home, I heard the Lord tell me to go now and visit my mother and love on her as He loved on me, so I obeyed and headed to Peabody. When I arrived, her kitchen table was covered with glue, paper, markers, and a mess really. She told me she was making Christmas cards for her children, grandchildren, and great-grandchildren. That scene filled my heart with love for her, and I began to cry. She said she had just prayed to God and asked Him to send me to her house so that I could help her write out her creations. Her hands were in much arthritic pain that she could not sign the cards. Of course, I would help her, I said, and she cried out to God, thanking Him for His faithfulness in sending me to her. We had dinner together after that, and we both went to the prayer meeting at church. It was such an anointed meeting, and she put her head on my shoulder and rubbed my back as she said she loved me and loved her God as she thanked Him for sending me to her that day. He healed our hearts that night and we gave Him all the praise, honor and glory. Mom joined the Crochet and Pray group while I attended my Healing Prayer Group; and we were blessed to go together every week. We became such great friends, and to this day, I thank God for healing our hearts. Hallelujah, and praise God forevermore! These are the times I will always treasure as I remember my beautiful mother and the work God did in both of our hearts in her later years. Especially now that my hands are in pain due to arthritis, I remember her with so much love and compassion. It is so difficult to lose a parent. Even though we will spend eternity together, it still hurts.

- My Body Gets Attacked

My body gets attacked at my yearly check-up. My doctor examined me and said my heart was beating too fast and my blood pressure was too high. She immediately called an ambulance and I was transferred to Lahey Hospital in Burlington. I was diagnosed with a mild heart attack and A Fib. They wanted me to have a Cardio version Procedure; I was then filled with more fear and stress. I can recall one day when I had tubes in me on both arms and felt so helpless and scared. A phlebotomist came into my room at 4:00 a.m. to take blood that morning, and I begged him to leave because I just wanted to die. Instead, he asked me if the Bible on my chest was mine.

I said, "Yes, but I have no hands free to read it, but I know God is in my heart and that He is blessing me in spite of all this pain and suffering."

He then asked me if he could read the book of Jonah to me. He knelt by my bed and began to read it to me. He was so gentle that I truly thought he was an angel sent by God and maybe my time was up to take me home. He prayed for me and told me that God had a bigger plan for me and I couldn't die, but I needed to rest and be still and know that God is in control of my life. He told me to pray and ask God why I was here in the hospital. Then God spoke to me because Jonah disobeyed God and ran from going to Nineveh to bring His Word to God's people and Jonah ended up in the mouth of a whale. So now I was asking God, "Why am I here, what did I do or not do?"

"Oh, God, forgive me for my disobedience in not writing the book," I prayed. There seemed to always be roadblocks prohibiting me from obeying God and writing this book.

I left the hospital that Sunday, and I immediately headed to my church in Lynnfield. I went in the back prayer room where the pastor was praying with his staff before he went into the sanctuary to preach. I walked into the prayer group and asked them to lay hands on me because I just came from Lahey Hospital with a diagnosis of a minor heart attack and a-fib. I asked if they would pray for me. Of course, they did. The pastor also took me before the congregation, and he had the entire church pray for me. I believed I was healed at that moment.

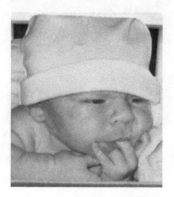

The very next day, my daughter called me and told me that she was with child. I cried like a baby and told her how I just left the hospital and I went to my church and how they all prayed for me. And now I was going to be a Grammy; that was my gift from God, and I made a commitment that day to stay healed and believe God that I would live and not die to see my first grandchild (Psalm 118:17). I then prayed that God would give me a grandson, and my daughter said she would name him Will, and that meant to us that God's will be done in my life. William was born in July, and he became the joy of my life, and I thanked God for giving me a reason to live when I wanted to give up. I thoroughly enjoyed babysitting for him every Sunday and Monday until he started school. We were bonded for life with the greatest memories of love. Hallelujah!

- My Mother-in-Law's Testimony

Now I would love to share Lillian's testimony, who was my mother-in-law. Lillian came to live in Massachusetts from Florida when her husband passed away. My husband was to be her caregiver, and she took residence at the Herrick House to be close to my husband's office. He was able to visit her on a daily basis and was close enough in case of an emergency. After a couple of years, Lillian took ill and needed to be transferred to Beverly Hospital. Eventually, she went into a coma, and I continued to visit her and pray over her, sing to her, and read the Bible to her. She really had no other visitors except me and my husband and occasionally her grandchildren. I was told that she was not a likable person, and they often avoided her. But when she moved to Beverly and entered that facility, everyone called her Silly Lilly! Her personality completely changed, and everyone loved her. Eventually, her condition grew worse after many TIAs, and she then became comatose. One day, when I was visiting her, I noticed that all the machines were no longer attached to her body. I panicked, and I went home to pray and asked God what I should do. Then I asked my husband why he allowed that. I told him that God specifically told me in prayer that she had not accepted Jesus Christ yet, and she was not to have the machines turned off. She hadn't been connected to the machines for over a week; so I convinced him to have her hooked up as God told me to do so immediately! So I continued to visit her and pray, read, and sing to her while she was in that coma.

Now it was Sunday, and my girlfriends and I were planning to go out to lunch after the church service, but suddenly my heart was not at peace. I went into the ladies' room to pray and ask God why I had no peace. God clearly told me to go home and pray in the Holy Spirit for Lillian for exactly two hours. I told my friends I needed to leave immediately as I had an emergency at home. I obeyed God and prayed in my prayer room until the Lord specifically told me to go and visit Lillian. My husband was hunting in New Hampshire that week, and it was now over a week since she had been hooked back up to the breathing machines. When I got to the hospital and entered her room, I told her I loved her, and suddenly her eyes began to open. The strange thing was that she was facing me, but her eyes were looking over my head behind me, and she was smiling. I was a bit concerned, and when I spoke, she continued to look over my head and behind me, as if someone taller was standing there. I got glory bumps all over me and was even afraid to turn around to see who was there. She then began calling out to Him…"Jesus, Jesus," and kept smiling. She finally looked at me with that most beautiful smile and said she was ready to invite Jesus into her heart. Talk about glory bumps. I tell you, it was a miracle above all miracles.

After praying and inviting Jesus into her heart and asking God to forgive her of all her sins, she told me that she was not a very nice person in her life and she was so sorry. I told her that God forgave her, and she cried like a baby. In fact, we both did, as we embraced each other with love. Then she said she was hungry, so I called the nurse, who was so excited when she saw Lilly. She brought her a turkey dinner, and she ate the entire dinner, including the dessert. All the nurses loved "Silly Lilly" and were so happy for her. I excused myself while she was eating her dessert, and I ran out to the hall and called my husband, who was hunting up north. "Please come home immediately and be with your mother because this could be your last opportunity to love and comfort her!"

I told him what God told me and of all that transpired that day with his mother and how she accepted Jesus Christ as her Lord. I realized that Len did not understand godly things at that time, but I still begged him to trust me that I heard from God and to please come home now. Well, he did show up two hours later, and when he did, I left the room so that the two of them would be alone. When I peeked into the room, they were both crying and hugging each other. That night while they were embracing each other, she closed her eyes for the last time and went home to heaven to be with her Lord and Savior. Watching a soul surrender her life to Jesus Christ is the greatest miracle I have ever witnessed. I will praise God forevermore.

All praise to God Who turns all things around for the good to those who are called and who love Him. I will tell you that with much prayer and intercession, Len will finally submit to the Lord's call to join the family of God very soon!

- God Answers My Prayers To Initiate A Nursing Home Ministry Under The Auspices Of Calvary Christian Church

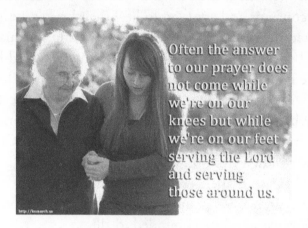

Often the answer to our prayer does not come while we're on our knees but while we're on our feet serving the Lord and serving those around us.

Nursing Home Ministry

I shared my vision with the senior pastor of my church and he was blessed to offer me the leadership position of the Nursing Home Ministry at CCC. Our vision was to recruit compassionate volunteers from our church, offer them weekly meetings with prayer and intercession, and to equip them to meet the spiritual and emotional needs of the residents in long-term Health Care facilities in the North Shore. Our goal was to train, mentor, and support men and women to adopt a health care facility in their community, and to commit to visit these facilities on a weekly basis. Also, we wanted to discover the great treasures hidden behind every sacrifice given in His love so that His will would be done in each health-care facility to the glory and honor of our Father God in heaven. We wanted to share God's love, hope, peace and joy to all. Our great mission would bridge the gap between our church and the residents, and to develop friendships with the residents so that we could provide them with spiritual care, encouragement, and love.

In our pursuit, God allowed us to share Jesus with the residents in so many ways. We offered praise and worship events, Bible messages, and provided the residents an opportunity to accept Jesus Christ as their Lord and Savior. We wanted to listen to their concerns and ask God to heal their broken hearts, hear their cry for help, and meet their emotional and spiritual needs. We also believed that our God who lives in us, would bring to them the light, the peace, and joy that they need to thrive and survive without their families and loved ones. We celebrated their birthdays with small gifts, snacks and love. During holidays we brought homemade gifts and treats, and at Christmas time, the children from our church sang Christmas Carols and blessed them with their child-like faith and love. We offered monthly church services and served Holy Communion as well. God's blessings and love abounded to all!

Here are more of the testimonies that I will treasure for the rest of my life.

Nursing Home Testimonies

- Hear the Heart of Nursing Home Residents

You may be asking by now why these nursing home testimonies are important to share with others. I would have thought the same once upon a time, before I got a letter from an old woman as she shared her broken heart. I will tell you some of what she said that changed my life forever. And when I prayed, God sent me on a mission to the nursing homes to fill me with His compassion to go and tell them just how much He loved His children who unfortunately were sent there at the end of their life.

You see, their life has run its course and in the blinking of an eye, they are there left alone. Some once had a husband or a wife that they loved with all their heart, children for whom they spent their entire lives caring for, but where are those children now? They are too busy with their own lives to go and visit their parents and grandparents. So they sit alone in a room with a TV on that they care nothing about but pray to God for some contact with a loved one and a touch of their hand and feel the love in their heart. They think now no one cares that they love juice with their meals or that they can't even feed themselves unless someone comes along and helps them. Sometimes they are so hungry but can't even hold a fork, and no one helps them, so they go to bed hungry day after day. Does anyone care that they once could shampoo their own hair and shower themselves and dress with clean clothes? But if their aide doesn't show up one day, those services never happen. Will someone take them outside for some fresh air that they long to feel the warm breezes on their face, or to hear the birds chirping again, or to see the beautiful blue sky? They once loved to go to church, but now they cannot even remember the joys of praising God and hear a sermon preach the Good News that brought life and healing to their flesh.

"Have you hugged your kids today?" a famous saying goes, but has anyone hugged an aging parent or grandparent today? If their lips are chapped, who will bring them ChapStick or even care that their throat is dry and their lips are cracked? So here they are, left alone in a strange place, stuck in front of TV that they despise, with a broken heart and a life almost over and a heart crying out for someone to care for them and love them. That is why it is so important to go and tell these lonely people that God is alive and loves them very much.

Can we at least be the bible they may have never read? So when you read these testimonies know how much these people were loved, cared for, and shown the love of God; and remember that they too will now spend eternity with a loving God forevermore. Hopefully they will remember you and the love you shared with them once upon a time!

- Testimony of Ms. Martha at a Nursing Facility

Ms. Martha was one of my dearest and most lovely friends I visited twice a week. She loved the Lord so much. She was a prayer warrior, and we loved to pray together for the needs of all the patients and their families. She loved God so much that we enjoyed sharing the mighty miracles He did in that facility. They were all like family helping each other, tailoring each other's clothes, praying for one another, and bringing joy and love to all.

Ms. Martha also owned many beautiful collectible dolls, and her room always felt like home—warm, cozy, and safe. We loved praying for our families, our children, and our grandchildren so that they would know and love our Lord Jesus Christ. As the years went on, Ms. Martha's health was failing, and she needed more assistance with normal routines like eating and dressing. The greatest gift for Ms. Martha was when her daughter Caroline and her oldest grandson gave their lives to Jesus Christ—what a celebration that was as we praised God for that miracle. She was so happy and the Pastor visited her at the facility as she became a member of Calvary Christian Church. Soon thereafter Ms. Martha went home to heaven and she was missed by all. The awesome part of this testimony is that I get to see her family at church every week which blesses my soul; and that always keeps Ms. Martha's memory close to my heart. God is so good all of the time and I thank you Lord for Ms. Martha.

- Testimony of My Mom's Dear Friend

I visited her only by accident as I visited her roommate every week. She was a new tenant, shall I say. She did look familiar to me, so I went to ask her if she perhaps knew me.

I introduced myself, and she told me that she was my mother's dearest friend, a friend who lived down the street from my mom. She told me how she wanted to go home and if I could ask my God to bless her with that request. So I asked her if she wanted to know more about my God, and she agreed. We talked for a couple of hours, and she then asked me if I could pray with her for a deeper relationship with Jesus Christ. Of course, that is my goal when I visit with the residents, and I was happy to pray with her. I visited her weekly, and she continued to get better, and we prayed that God would let her go home since she progressed so rapidly. My mom started to come with me to visit her, and that made Sally so happy. Within a couple of months, she was healed and able to go home, and we praised God! After she settled in at home, she asked me if she could go and minister with me to the nursing home, and I was happy to comply. My mom and her friend visited the nursing home with me, and it was a blessing to have helpmates to bring the joy and peace of the Lord to that facility.

• Testimony of Ms. Helen at the Nursing Home

A fellow prayer warrior called me today and asked me if I could visit a patient who was the mother of her tax accountant. She was dying in a nursing home. I asked where she was, and she told me she was at a nursing facility that I frequented. Of course, I asked my friend for more information and I agreed to visit with her. When she gave me the patient's name, I almost fell over. You see, Ms. Helen was my neighbor all my life since childhood. My friend told me that Ms. Helen had Alzheimer's disease and that she might not remember me. But I was so excited now to visit her. I then asked where Ms. Helen's sons were living so that I could visit with them as well. They were all good friends years ago, and I even went to school with them.

You see, Ms. Helen was my mom's best friend for years, but my mom was already in heaven with Jesus, so I would not have known unless God let me know. I prayed for Ms. Helen for two more days until God gave me the opportunity to go and visit her. When I entered her room, she was sleeping peacefully, and she was as beautiful at age ninety as ever before. I gently held her hand and began singing "Jesus Loves You" to her. Then I recited Psalm 23 to her because I know that people that are in a coma can still hear everything that is said. Then I saw her lips starting to move, and she started reciting the Psalm along with me. Now I was singing "Bless the Lord Oh My Soul," and she began singing as well, and she started to open her eyes staring at me. She now was holding my hand tightly and thanking Jesus for sending her the angel that He promised to send her. Now I was reciting Psalm 91, and she was completely awake and looking behind me, talking to Jesus. She told Him how much she loved Him and needed to sing all her praises to Him, and she prayed to hear His Word again. She kept telling Jesus how thankful she was for fulfilling His promises to her with such peace and joy on her face. Finally, the nurse entered the room and recognized me because we attended the same church. She too was so blessed to see Ms. Helen praising God and out of the comatose state. I visited Helen for a couple more weeks until one day Jesus took her home. I attended her services where I met my old school friends and told them how she came out of the coma and praised God! I let her family know that we prayed to God together, and she was so happy to go home with Jesus Whom she loved. They were all so blessed, and they were crying happy tears, knowing that their mom was in heaven and one day we would all see each other again. I was able to share Ms. Helen's testimony with everyone at her wake, and many came to know Jesus Christ and were blessed. All praise, glory, and honor go to our Father, Son, and Holy Spirit Who leads and guides us to all truth. Hallelujah! God is moving so graciously at the nursing homes, and I am forever blessed!

- Ms. Pam's Testimony of the Power of Prayer at the Nursing Home

It is amazing how God knows who needs a touch from Jesus, which nursing home to visit, and prepares their hearts before I knock on the door.

One day He led me to this nursing home and told me to bring the *Evangel Magazine* that I got from church. I tell you, I was just as surprised as the patient when I see how God is so faithful and with perfect timing. I popped into her room, introducing myself, with this magazine in my hand. She got so excited because she was bored and always loved reading her *Evangel Magazine* from her church. And here I come with that magazine and with no clue why I brought it with me. Because she was extremely overweight, she was unable to get out of bed and had always been neglected by her family. She had no contact from them, but she especially missed her mother, who had rejected her. She had been living at this facility for a few years and was so heartbroken and depressed. She loved Jesus and asked me to join my faith with hers and asked God to bring her mother back into her life and help her lose weight. She thought maybe then her mom would take her home again. So every week, we joined hands and humbly gave our requests to God. After many months of prayers and believing God, her social worker contacted Ms. Pam's mom, and she did come to visit her. In November, Ms. Pam's mom took her home to live with her after many years of separation and a broken heart. Ms. Pam was so happy and praising God, and she said it was a miracle she would remember for the rest of her life. She was now reconciled with her long-lost family. Hallelujah.

- Ms. Anna's Testimony at the Nursing Home

One warm summer day, I visited a frail and tiny woman sitting by the door so sad and forlorn, and I just wanted to take her into my arms and love on her. I asked if she would like some company, and she gladly accepted. She began telling me that she had no family left and felt so alone, depressed, and afraid to die alone in that place where no one cared. She lost her husband many years ago and was never blessed with any children or a family. She had all these questions about dying, she said. Who would know when it happened, and where would they put her? I told her about Jesus Christ and how much He loved her and that He didn't want her to worry because He had her in the palm of His hands. She did not know Jesus and asked if I could tell her all about Him and how to invite Him into her lonely world. I was so happy to share Jesus Christ with Ms. Anna, and we talked for hours on end. When her heart was ready, she gladly accepted Jesus Christ, and she held my hands so tight while she repented of all her sins. After she prayed, she let go of my hands like a little angel and lifted them up to God, thanking Him for saving her life and for loving her. Ms. Anna's salvation was so genuine and precious; I will remember that moment forever. We sang "Amazing Grace" and "How Great Thou Art," and she kept thanking God for visiting her and sending her an angel of light.

We became good friends as I visited her twice a week so that we could pray together and bring her the peace and love she needed. She was so weak and frail that I even had to feed her when I was there and prayed for an aide to feed her and care for her in my absence. I even took her outside for fresh air. As we walked around the facility, she could hear the birds singing, smell the flowers, and feel the fresh air on her face. She was like a little child seeing life for the first time in years. Ms. Anna was so happy when I took her outdoors for fresh air. She would sing "Amazing Grace" and tell everyone that an angel from God has come to visit her. Even the nurses and the staff kept singing "Amazing Grace" every time they came into her room. They sang it to her before she closed her eyes at night too. She even came to the Bible studies with me, and she always encouraged the other residents to join her so God would set them free.

When it was time for Ms. Anna to meet her Maker, I arranged for her to be laid at a beautiful funeral home in Salem, and she was laid in her casket on pink satin sheets adorned with beautiful pink flowers from her Lord Jesus Christ. When I was at her service, no one else was present, and I wished her farewell in Jesus's name. I knew that she was surrounded by many angels that day as they escorted her home to heaven. What a beautiful angel Ms. Anna was, and I will love her forever! Thank You, Jesus, for taking her home and loving her more than she had ever known!

- Nurse Sam's Testimony at a Nursing Facility

I was coming to the nursing home this day to bring a Bible that I promised to a resident. All the patients were in the dining room when I got there, almost ready for dinner. I would love to visit at dinnertime so that I could pray over the food before they ate, and patients loved to thank God before meals. While they were eating, I started reading the Psalms to them when a male nurse came running up to me saying he loved that Bible so much and if he could have it. I was a bit surprised that he was so forward about it, and I told him it was a gift for a patient there. He begged me if he could have it because his was lost or stolen from his locker, and he said he needed his Bible and could not live without it. Of course, I could understand that, so I asked the patient, and she obliged, and I told her that I would order her another one when I got home. I know how he must have felt because I would be devastated if I lost my Bible. It's like holding on to Jesus himself. He kept thanking us and just held it to his heart as he wept with joy. After my rounds, as I was walking down the hall to leave the facility, there he was on his break, reading his Bible. When I continued to walk by him, he asked me if I was calling his name. I said, "No, but maybe Jesus was."

He believed God was calling, "Samuel, Samuel," and was overwhelmed with joy! I then shared with him that God wanted me to have services at that facility, and he said he would be happy to help me set it up with management and he would help me in any way he could. He did as he promised, and in no time, we held monthly services with praise and worship, Bible studies, and serving Holy Communion. The pastors at my church made a commitment to preach once a month and serve communion. The outcome was amazing, and so many residents gave their lives to Jesus Christ.

God is moving in many ways at this nursing home, and I am blessed to be a part of God's miracle working power.

- Ms. Maureen's Testimony at the Nursing Home

Oh, how everyone loved Ms. Maureen, who sat by the front door and was ready to meet me no matter what time of day it was. If she wasn't at the front door waiting, she sat by the elevators. She was truly a blessing as she praised God in all her waking hours. She loved to pray with me, and we would go to other rooms and pray for whoever needed prayer. We would go around the floors singing praise songs to other residents, and they too would join us in praising God. She always believed God was talking to her and loving her as she loved Him with all her heart, soul, mind, and body. Ms. Maureen loved the Bible studies, receiving Communion, and always participated in the praise and worship times in our church services. She was an amazing woman with great faith and love for Jesus. I will miss her, and I look forward to the day when we will join our faith and love with Jesus in heaven for all eternity!

- Testimony of the Wounded Warrior at the Nursing Home

I visited a young man I will call the Wounded Warrior being of a strong stature but bedridden and depressed. I knocked at his door and asked if I could visit with him. He was reluctant at first, but he said yes, I could stay a few minutes. We talked awhile, and I asked him how he came to be at a nursing home. His leg was amputated during his duty in the Gulf War. He began to tell me that he just wanted to die because his wife and children left him and the loneliness and pain was too much for him to deal with. I asked if I could pray for him, but he declined. I asked if I could at least visit him again, and he replied, "Maybe." I left the nursing home that day with a great burden in my heart for the veterans who have fought to protect our country. My wounded warrior friend began to trust me as I visited him a couple times a week, and he eventually allowed me to pray with him and for him. I convinced him one day to get out of the bed, and I would take him outdoors for some fresh air. The nurse got us a wheelchair, and he complied. He loved being outdoors, and we became friends; he trusted me and, I was able to take him outside often.

One day I asked him what else I could do for him. He smiled and said he would love an Italian submarine sandwich. I smiled and said, "Okay, I'll be back soon," and out I went to the local sandwich shop. When I returned, you would think I brought him a pot of gold. After a few weeks, I convinced him to consider getting a prosthesis, and he said he would think about it. And yes, his social worker got him an appointment, and yes, he got one. He began to practice to walk with a crutch.

He was getting set free and less depressed. He was happy and excited to walk on his own, and soon we would pray for his family to take him home. He became more confident and less depressed, dressing himself, shaving, and making himself presentable. He actually waited for my weekly visits with such joy and excitement. One day he asked me to pray with him because he was ready to hear about the Good News of Jesus Christ and what Jesus has done for him. Prayer became a joy for him now, and he actually started to have faith that God had a plan for him and his hope was being restored. After almost a year, the Wounded Warrior prayed, asking God to bring his wife and children back. That was amazing, and I will end this testimony by saying that the Wounded Warrior got his prayers answered. It was the day when he was almost running down the hall with his crutch and a smile bigger than you could imagine. Because His wife and kids were picking him up and taking him home to live with them forever. I can cry with the memory of God's amazing grace, love, and joy. Miracles do happen in the nursing homes, and I give God all glory, honor, and praise!

> The Lord your God is living among you.
> He is a mighty savior. He will take delight
> in you with gladness. With His love, He will
> calm all your fears. He will rejoice over you
> with joyful songs! (Zephaniah 3:17)

- The Fireman's Testimony at the Nursing Home

I was making my daily rounds at the nursing home, and I stopped to visit Ms. A. You must know that some of these residents have never had a visitor nor been touched by another human being.

I would wheel my little cart around while making my rounds as I walked through the facility. My cart was filled with moisture creams, toothbrushes, books, magazines, game books, Bibles, candy bars, and many more items. I was in Ms. A's room rubbing her arms, legs, and feet when the fragrance drew this fireman to her room, and he knocked on the door.

"What is that coconut smell? I love it," he asked.

We invited him in, and that's when I met the fireman and we became friends. He too eventually got blessed as he attended our Bible services and fellowships. He invited Jesus Christ into his heart, and he really appreciated the church services at the nursing home. The reason why he lived there was that he had fallen off a high ladder and broke his leg and, he severely hurt his back which, was not healing properly. His prayer was to be healed and leave the nursing home for good. We played games and shared his dreams and prayers to eventually go home. After about a year and much prayer, he too left the facility. The nice memory I hold dear to my heart is that Mr. Fireman calls my family every holiday and birthday with his blessings, wishes, and love.

• Mr. Jim's Testimony at a Nursing Facility

Mr. Jim was just the opposite of Ms. Maureen, who always wanted to hear the Good News. Jim sat by the elevators, but he did not want to talk about Jesus. So every time I came to visit, I would offer Mr. Jim a *Sports Illustrated* magazine to read, and he loved candy bars. I was always available to pray for Jim, but only if he was ready. Regardless, we still became good friends. But he was pretty adamant and did not want to hear about God. I would bless him and assured him that God loved him and so did I. He had been living there for quite some time with diabetes, with no family to care for him, and with cancer in the toes, losing one along with knee problems, so he was unable to walk.

About a year later, I was ready to go up to the second floor when he came to me asking if I would come and talk with him when I finished making my rounds. "Of course," I said and headed up to the second floor.

Suddenly, I heard the voice of God in the elevator very clearly tell me to go back downstairs and see what was on Mr. Jim's heart. I obeyed and headed back down. We went to a private place where he asked me if my church had a recovery program.

"Yes, of course," I said, "in fact they are meeting tomorrow night. Would you be interested to go?"

I immediately called one of my male volunteers who would be happy to pick Mr. Jim up at five thirty, and he told Jim he would even take him to dinner first. He humbly asked me for a Bible, so I ran to my car shocked and thanking God. I brought him a new Bible. I prayed with him and told him I would see him soon and to enjoy reading his Bible. I stopped by the nursing home the next day, and there was Mr. Jim learning how to walk with a walker on a ninety-five-degree-hot day and said he was determined to go to the recovery program that night and he would walk in there no matter what. That evening I came to church for the women's Bible prayer meeting. Around eight thirty, I was getting restless and slipped out of the prayer meeting. As I was walking down the church steps, there was my volunteer with Mr. Jim driving by, and they stopped to tell me that Jim gave his life to Jesus Christ. I wept with excitement and did my victory dance while Mr. Jim told me that if I were not at the nursing home yesterday, he was planning on taking his life. We all rejoiced, praising God for His perfect timing. Then Mr. Jim told me that he was not receiving his benefit checks from SSDI in over a year. The next day I took Mr. Jim's situation and met with a woman who deals with Social Security at NSES, and we began the investigation. Within two weeks, he received his past-due checks, giving Mr. Jim hope that he could one day leave the nursing home where he thought he would live for the rest of his life. That meant Mr. Jim would not have to submit his entire check to the nursing home, we prayed now for an apartment for him. I shopped around and found him an apartment a stone's throw from our church, which meant he could walk to church every day if he so desired. And that was what he did.

Jim was an available servant working at the church wherever and whenever he was needed. We found him furniture that was donated to him by my good friend, and people from our church donated sheets, blankets, towels, and a kitchen set along with many items for his kitchen. It was so beautiful, and all the glory went to our Lord! He was able to walk again and become so independent and so full of joy and peace. He then got trained in the nursing home ministry, and he became the greatest helpmate ever! He became my assistant and was as helpful as he gave of his time. He was a blessing to me and to this ministry. He enjoyed visiting his friends at the nursing home and sharing the love of Jesus with them, as well as joining the hospitality ministry and the prison ministry. He was committed to telling the world about His Jesus Who brought him life, freedom, and peace for the first time in his life. He was a blessing to all, and the world missed Mr. Jim when God took him home to heaven a few years later. We will all miss Mr. Jim, and he was loved by all his friends from church and from the nursing home.

- Testimony of an Old Friend in the Nursing Home

I was making my rounds when one of the residents that I visited weekly told me she was going to the second floor to visit her son's grandmother. She asked me if I could come along and perhaps pray for her. I agreed, and when I walked into the room and saw her name, I almost fell over. Can you recall when my family moved out of the city to a farm in the North Shore over sixty years ago? Well, the resident I was visiting is the gal whose family owned the farm where we grew up together. The ambulance suddenly appeared to transport her to Salem Hospital because she stopped breathing. She was suffering from chronic obstructive pulmonary disease and pneumonia from the severe results of smoking and alcoholism. I prayed for her that night, and on Saturday morning, God told me to visit her at the hospital. I was shocked when I entered her room as she was not even eighty pounds and looked more like ninety than sixty-seven years old. I wept and noticed her beautiful blue eyes though and remembered that she was one of the most beautiful women I had ever known when I was but a kid. She opened her eyes and remembered me instantly, even calling me by my maiden name. We embraced, cried, and loved on each other. I told her about my ministry and what happened yesterday when I was at the nursing home and that I was going to visit her. She held my hands tightly and asked me to pray for her, which I did willingly. She accepted Jesus Christ into her heart and cried tears of joy, knowing that she would go home and be with Jesus in heaven forever. I promised that I would visit her often and prayed and believed God would heal her.

Within days, the Lord took her home to heaven, and we attended her wake and funeral. She died on the seventeenth, and the number of our home on the farm was number 17. And the next strange thing was that her daughter was my husband's employee for a few years, and we never knew she was her daughter.

I will never forget this testimony and how God orders our steps and how there are no accidents with Him. He prepares our steps if we are obedient to listen to His small, still voice. I was so sad to see her leave at such a young age, but I will remember her, and I thanked God for letting our paths meet again after so many years. I was at the right place at the right time, thanks to God Who orders my steps. But I am more thankful for her salvation! Hallelujah!

> I have observed something else under the sun. The fastest runner doesn't always win the race, and the strongest warrior doesn't always win the battle. The wise sometimes go hungry, and the skillful are not necessarily wealthy. And those who are educated don't always lead successful lives. It is all decided by chance, by being in the right place at the right time. (Ecclesiastes 9:11)

• Ms. Carol's Testimony at the Nursing Home

Let me tell you how I met Ms. Carol at the Nursing Home in 2011. I was doing my rounds on three floors, and I would knock on patients' doors and ask if I can visit with them, but her door was always closed, and she would say, "Go away," whenever I knocked. I never would force myself on anyone. One day I prayed and asked God how I could get her to invite me into her room.

Then I had an idea. I knocked, opened the door a bit, and said, "Hi, do you know that we have the same name?" I then asked her if she knew what Carol meant.

She said, "No, but I sure would like to know."

"Can I come in and tell you?" I asked.

She replied, "Okay, you can come in."

I told her our name meant song of joy and that I loved to sing and praise God. I asked her if I could sing her a song, and she agreed and joined me while I was singing "Amazing Grace." We harmonized so perfectly that we both laughed and agreed that we should keep singing, and that was what we did; that was how we became friends. I told her about the Bible studies I had at the facility and that we sang and praised God and then we had fellowship and refreshments. She agreed to join me the next time I came to the nursing home. I asked her why she was there, being so young, and she told me that she fell and broke her hip at the shelter where she lived. I told her I would be there next week for the Bible study and would come to get her in her room. We parted joyfully and were happy to have finally met each other.

The following week, I went to get her in her room, but the bed was empty, and the room was cleaned out. I was so sad because the nurses would not tell me where she lived due to the HIPPA laws. After we held our Bible study, I left in a hurry so I could pray and ask God where Carol lived. I prayed in my car and gave my frustration to the Lord and asked Him to please find her for me.

The following week I had my appointment at physical therapy on Route 1 in Danvers. I was lying on the table, and my therapist was working on my shoulder due to a rotator cuff tear. Then she told me to squeeze the ball between my legs, so as surprised as I was, I looked up and said, "I thought you were working on my shoulder?"

She laughed and answered, "Oh, not you, the other Carol next to you."

I immediately looked up, and it was Ms. Carol from he Nursing Home. I screamed, excused myself, and jumped off the table and cried out to her in shock. I told her that I had been looking all over for her since last week. She said they sent her back to her shelter, and she had no way to find me to let me know. But I told her I prayed and trusted God Who knows everything about us. And sure enough, we were at the same facility on the same day. We screamed and hugged and then we exchanged telephone numbers. She gave me her address, and I told her I would come visit her that week at the shelter. She agreed to come to church with me the following Sunday. Now what are the chances of seeing her at my PT in Danvers when she lives in Lynn. We believed it was a divine intervention from our awesome God. Even our therapist agreed that only God could arrange that appointment for us to meet at PT. We all gave the glory to God as we praised Him.

I visited the shelter a few days later, and I was so upset with her living conditions. There were alcoholics, drug addicts, heavy-duty cigarette smokers, big burly men calling her names, and they were obnoxious to her. She was undernourished, losing her hair, extremely thin, and hardly ate. My heart was broken, and I prayed to God to show me how to get her out of that shelter. She had been in the shelter for eleven years after her husband left her off in the street, divorced her, and sold their house. Needless to say, she was devastated, depressed, and very scared. She had not seen nor heard from him or her son since he dropped her off and left her on the street. Police found her and placed her in that shelter.

After much prayer and intercession for her, I had heard about a private home in Salem where they provide housing for homeless women. It was a warm and loving environment across from Salem Harbor. I scheduled an appointment for us to go for an interview, and they too agreed that she had to get out of the shelter in Lynn. They gladly accepted her as a permanent resident. We were ecstatic, and I began to get the ball rolling. I found people to donate furniture for her new private room, I hired a few strong men from the church who helped me transport her belongings from Lynn to Salem; and we set her up in a beautiful room with a magnificent view of the ocean. And that was how God treated Ms. Carol, like a queen, and He loved on her like never before.

She moved in on her sixtieth birthday, and we had a special birthday party in her honor. She loved her new home. She had put on weight, and she enjoyed her newfound freedom in Christ. She wanted her own telephone but had no money, so my husband agreed to get her a phone and pay her Comcast monthly bill. We both were blessed so that we could stay in touch. Carol was so happy and blessed that all was working out for her in her life. I now had an open door to minister to other women in this facility, and many gave their hearts to Jesus Christ as well. God is just so amazing. He actually takes my breath away when I think about all He has done for Ms. Carol and others in that facility. I am Carol's health-care proxy to this day as she is living a beautiful and fulfilling life at a home for Women, which truly is a mansion on earth facing the beautiful harbor.

One more note about Carol... I visited her to celebrate her birthday on December 15, the week before I left to spend the winter in Florida. It is the date of my mom's death, so I will always remember Carol's birthday. While we were visiting, she asked me where I was going in Florida, because she had a cousin who also lived in Florida. Of course, I thought Florida was such a huge state. I sure doubted Carol would even know where it was. I told her that we also owned a home in Florida and when she got her cousin's address, I realized that we lived only a few blocks away. Now, what are the chances of that. She looked in her desk and said, "Here, I will even show you a photograph of her." Now, know that Carol had only one relative in this entire world, and it was her cousin in Florida.

When I arrived in Florida, I sent her cousin a note to introduce myself and the reason for the note. Then I called her the next week, and I was surprised that she sounded just like Carol over the phone. We were excited to meet each other at church the following Sunday. I cannot stop thinking of how God is so absolutely amazing, and it is more than I can think or imagine. Here it is nine years later, and God is still blessing Carol with His miracle working power.

Now all glory to God, who is able,
through his mighty power at work within us,
to accomplish infinitely more than we might
ask or think. Glory to him in the church and

in Christ Jesus through all generations for-ever and ever! Amen. (Ephesians 3:20)

- Mr. Sandi's Testimony at Nursing Home

This is a story about my dearest friend Donna who was a hospice nurse who visited many patients in the same nurs-ing homes that I frequented. She, being a prayer warrior like myself, would let me know which patients were coming to the end of their lives so that I could join her to pray for them, and Mr. Sandi was one of them.

I visited Mr. Sandi often, especially if he called me because he needed me to pray with him. I always brought him his favorite magazine or a candy bar, and we became close friends. He loved Jesus and was comfortable talking about his condition, and he knew when his time was up, Jesus would take him home, leaving him fearless. He was a Harley man, and he really missed riding his bike, but still he never complained. He had the sweetest dis-position, and he loved sharing his heroic biking stories. This par-ticular day, he was depressed, and I seldom saw him like that, so I asked him what was wrong. He said he was not afraid to meet his

Maker but wondered how to ask the Lord a couple of questions that troubled him. So I told him I would sit and pray with him as he talked with God because prayer is talking to God. I told him, "Whatever concerns him also concerns God, so let's join hands and pray and ask God to intervene for you." He asked God if he could get a knitted hat with the number 81 on it and wear it at his burial service. We joined hands and thanked God for his salvation and for making his wish come true. I then asked what 81 meant, and he told me it meant Hell's Angels. Of course, I was surprised and shocked, so I asked God if that was okay to ask that of Him, and I felt a peace and asked God to bless him. After I left his room, I visited other patients on the second floor. Then I got into the elevator to go to the third floor, but the elevator took me to the ground floor instead. I was about to get off the elevator and realized I needed to go back up when a big, strong, and burly-looking man entered the elevator. I stepped back in and introduced myself to him and told him I was the leader of the nursing home ministry at my church and asked him whom he was visiting. I noticed he was holding a knitted hat in his hand. He held it up to show me it had an "81" on the hat and said he felt God was telling him to bring this hat to a friend of his who was dying. He said that he hadn't seen him in a long time.

I suddenly screamed, saying, "Is that Mr. Sandi?"

And he said, "Yes, how did you know?"

I introduced myself to him just as the elevator stopped on the second floor. The door opened and I began to run down the hall to tell Mr. Sandi that God heard his prayers and his old friend was coming to see him. Just then, he entered the room with the hat, and Mr. Sandi began to cry and thank God for hearing his prayers so quickly. We all had a victory shout as we praised God together. I am so happy that God loves us so much that he even answers our simple prayers to meet our needs. What a blessed day for him as his friend wheeled him around the home and he told his friends how God blessed him, and he wore his 81 hat so proudly. I told Mr. Sandi that the "old man" who was once Hell's Angel would be buried six feet under, but the "new redeemed man" would be called "God's angel." God would be taking him to his heavenly home for all eternity, and that is the "Good News!"

I needed to say goodbye to Mr. Sandi because I was going on vacation for ten days to Florida, and I asked him to wait for me if he could and I would be back to see him soon. We shed tears and hugs, and I left that day for Florida. I was in Florida about six days now when I got a phone call from a nurse at that nursing home telling me that Mr. Sandi was ready to go to see his Maker in heaven. She asked me if I could talk with him so he could say goodbye to me, and she handed me the phone. I told Sandi that Jesus loved him more than anyone else, and I told him it was okay to leave to go to Jesus and that he did not need to wait for me. He thanked me and said he loved me. The nurse then took the phone and said he shed some tears and shut his eyes. She also said her phone never worked from the patients' rooms, and it was a miracle that today it worked so that I could say goodbye and set him free. I hung up, and I went out on the patio and cried like a baby. A man on the patio next to mine asked me if I was all right, and I told him why I was crying. He said he was a pastor and asked if he could pray for me and for my loss. I agreed, and he prayed the most beautiful prayer for Mr. Sandi and also that God would give me strength to let my friend go home. It was truly a blessing, and then he disappeared into his room. Later that day, I wanted to go to his room and thank him, but no one answered the door. I then went to see the desk clerk to inquire about the whereabouts of the pastor, and he said there was no pastor or anyone else in the room next to mine. "Hmmm," I thought, "could it have been an angel?" I believe it must have been!

You know, I really didn't want to leave for Florida, thinking it was letting Mr. Sandi down, but God showed me that it was okay in two ways. One was when we were walking out of the plane, I kept seeing pennies on the floor, and I stopped and picked them up, and God said, "Trust in God," and I smiled. Then when we got into the bus to go to Disney World, my granddaughter said, "Look, Grammy, up in the sky, the plane is sky-writing, and it says, 'Jesus loves you!'" That was my confirmation that God gave me permission to go on that vacation with my children and grandchildren and to enjoy them and love them as He loved us. I praised God the entire vacation!

It was my confirmation that I was in God's will

Family in Disney World

When I got home from that trip, I found out that Mr. Sandi's request was to not have the funeral until I returned. I was so happy, and the funeral was such a blessing with all his Hell's Angels present, and I got to share Mr. Sandi's testimony to all present, and God made a way for me to speak to the crowd and share Jesus Christ with them as Mr. Sandi wanted me to do. He told me to tell his friends that if they wanted to see him again and spend eternity with him, they must invite Jesus Christ into their hearts, and many did just that. It was a memorable event, and God got all the praise, glory, and honor.

I was told a few years later that another dear friend was in Florida on that same day and he took pictures of the sign in the sky that read "Jesus Loves You," and that was another confirmation from God that is where I needed to be. I sang hallelujah to my Lord as He always confirms His word to me!

• A Testimony of Forgiveness and Grace for the Policeman

This story began when I was a child living in Peabody, Massachusetts, and it ends full circle in a nursing home in the same city seventy years later. A teenage boy ran over my puppy when I was young girl, and he never stopped his car to inquire about my dog. My sister and I sat by our pet in the middle of the street on our little lawn chairs waiting all day for the police to arrive and take our dog off the street and bring him to the pound. I remember being so upset, sad, and broken. I never forgot this accident and always felt bitter and unforgiving toward this boy. The story continues when I was in high school and that same boy bragged in the cafeteria about a dog he ran over when he first got his license. I still remembered him, and now I was beginning to hate him. Time moved on, and when I gave my heart to Jesus, God reminded me of the bitterness I had in my heart for the boy who ran over my dog. So I had to repent and forgive that boy in my heart so that God can forgive me of my sins. "Forgive and you will be forgiven". (See Luke 6:37)

Years later, as I was driving to Salem and sitting in traffic, I noticed that the policeman who was directing traffic was that same boy who killed my dog years earlier. I felt that same pain in my heart as I recognized him. I immediately pulled my car over and ran to him in the middle of the street. I reminded him of the incident years ago when he ran over my dog and left the scene. Today I recognized him, and I told him I forgave him for killing my dog. The funny thing is, he remembered as well, and he accepted my apology and told me he was deeply sorry! I thought it strange that he actually became a policeman.

The story continues now as we come to this present day at a Nursing home where I ministered. I was visiting a woman and loving on her, reading the Bible to her and praying with her every week for healing. One day while visiting her, a policeman entered her room, and she introduced him to me as her son John. I was shocked that I was visiting his mother weekly, I didn't even realize that it was her son who killed my dog. We embraced, and he was as shocked as I was. His mom was so excited that I knew her son, and he was so excited that I visited and ministered to his mother. And the final end to this story is…how God is so good! Mr. Policeman's daughter now lives next-door to the house I was brought up in. Exactly where my dog was killed was in front of his daughter's house. This story definitely went full circle in my life. I give all the glory and honor to our Lord and Savior Jesus Christ.

- My Sweetest God Moment with Walter

I met Walter while on my rounds at a Nursing Facility. I was the leader of the nursing home ministry at Calvary Christian Church. Walter was ninety-four years of age and the sweetest and kindest man I had ever known. I was drawn to Walter by his sad eyes, his depression and loneliness since his wife of seventy years passed and he was the only survivor in his family. He would always sit in the great room, and he would keep to himself, looking so sad and alone. He had diabetes, heart issues, use of only one hand, and blind due to a stroke. Although he could never see me, he looked at me deeply as if he could. He would touch my curly hair and smell my perfume, and he recognized me immediately. I would tell him about Jesus and how much God loved him, and that always comforted Walter. I would sing songs to him as well, and one day he confessed to me that he loved Jesus, and he used to play the piano in the music ministry at his church for years before a stroke paralyzed his left side.

One dreary day, I asked him if I could push his wheelchair over to the piano and if he would praise God with me. He agreed, and before you knew it, he was playing the piano with one hand while I sang praise songs to Jesus. He amazed me so much that after that day, when I visited him, he would ask me to go to the piano so we could praise God. And the music we played drew many residents to the piano room, and we all praised God together. That turned his mourning into dancing and joy not only for us but for all the residents present. He now had come alive again, and I looked so forward to visiting him a couple of days a week.

About six months later, Walter came down with pneumonia and became very ill. He could only lie in his bed and sleep. I became sad as we loved praising God with the residents, and it always brought so much joy to him. One day, when I arrived, the nurse pulled me aside and told me Walter was ready to meet his Maker. I sobbed, and then I went into his room and knelt down beside his bed and began to touch his forehead and pray for him. He reached for me and began touching my hair and sniffing the air. He said God has sent him His angel with the curly hair, and he said he could smell her scent and now he could rest in peace. Then I remembered the scripture in 2 Corinthians 2:15–16.

> Our lives are a Christ-like fragrance rising up to God. But this fragrance is perceived

differently by those who are being saved and by those who are perishing. To those who are perishing, we are a dreadful smell of death and doom. But to those who are being saved, we are a life-giving perfume.

Walter then folded his hands over his heart and asked me to sing "Amazing Grace" to him. I did so willingly and humbly! Then he whispered softly that God had sent His angel to take him home to Jesus. I sobbed and told Him it was okay to go home to the Father Who was waiting for him, and I would meet him there someday when the Lord wills. My friend went home to be with Jesus that very day. We are not like many hucksters who preach for personal profit. We preach the Word of God with sincerity and with Christ's authority, knowing that God watches us. Hallelujah!

We are confident of all this because of our great trust in God through Christ. Not that we think we are qualified to do anything on our own but our qualification comes from God as He enables us to be ministers of His new covenant of His Holy Spirit which gives us life. (2 Corinthians 32:4)

I look forward to seeing Walter someday and spending forever with him in eternity. Hallelujah forevermore!

• Dot's Testimony at the Nursing Home

I made another important friend while I was visiting this nursing home, and we became friends as I visited her every week and brought my friends and family to meet her. She had been in that facility for over ten years because she was crippled and bedridden with rheumatoid arthritis. But that never stopped her from getting around in the nursing home and visiting others who were less fortunate than herself. She loved clothes, and every other day she would call "the ride" and go to various shopping malls in her motorized wheelchair. She was the greatest bargain hunter I have ever met. With her simple paycheck, she was always able to find the prettiest outfits at huge sales and markdowns. She often bought gifts for the other less fortunate residents as she loved to bless them. And she used her mangled hands to sew, knit, crochet, and create so many original items to sell to the people visiting the facility. She took orders from nurses, patients, those visiting the patients, and the nursing home staff. She lived in severe pain, but she was one of the most remarkable people I have ever met. She even put on craft shows in the facility for staff, patients, and their families, and everyone purchased gifts for the holidays. In November, she had such a huge success at her fair, selling knitted hats, mittens, socks, sweaters, blankets, bibs, and sweater sets for babies and children, along with various other handmade items.

One day, I set up a fair at my office at NSES and "the ride" brought her to our office from the nursing home. She sold so many items there that assured her of the spending money she needed to buy her supplies at Michael's and at other craft establishments. In fact, she made so much money at that fair that she was able to purchase a new sewing machine that was greatly needed. She also knitted covers for little pocket crosses and typed a loving message inside about Jesus Who loves His children. I purchased dozens of them to take to the people in other nursing homes that I visited. She called herself "the Crafty Lady," and she was a huge inspiration and a blessing to all who came to the nursing home. She also made angels and donated them to our Angel Tree at the church. God not only blessed her, but He blessed all the people who knew her, including me and my staff at church and my coworkers at NSES!

- Mr. Hugo's Testimony at the Nursing Home

The testimony of my deceased friend Mr. Hugo was one of my favorite memories ever, which proved to me that God loves and saves the good, the bad and the ugly! Whenever I visited that particular nursing home, I always passed his room because the door was closed and the other residents would tell me not to go into his room because the man was mean, bad, and ugly, and he might even throw me out or throw something at me if I entered his room. I was always hesitant to enter until one day I prayed to God and He told me to go and visit him. I was so surprised when I met him as his body was distorted with arthritis and the effects of spina bifida, and it was so sad to see him in that painful condition.

I introduced myself and told him I wanted to get to know him if he would give me the pleasure. He was gracious and kind, and as I looked at the pictures on his wall, he told me about his family and how very lonesome he was because his family had all died. He also shared with me that he was saddened that no one ever visited him. The pain he suffered also prohibited him to leave his room, he told me. It took him about two hours to tell me the story of his life and then apologized to me for doing all the talking. He then asked me about my life. I told him about my life with Jesus and all that He has done for me. He was so happy because no one ever told him the story of the birth of Christ and why He had to die on the cross. Before I had to leave, I asked him if he wanted to invite Jesus into his heart and make Him his Lord and Savior, and he responded, "Yes," which brought such joy to me. I left with a happy heart because he was so happy and blessed that he now knew Jesus and that Jesus loved him. He said he would never be lonesome again, and that blessed my soul. The next morning, I got a word from the Lord while I was in prayer telling me to go back to the nursing home, but I argued with God that it was too early to make my rounds and the nursing home preferred that the visitors come after 11:00 a.m. But the Holy Spirit persisted to grieve me until I obeyed Him. I finally obeyed His voice, and when I arrived, there was an ambulance parked out front. My heart started to beat heavy as I ran upstairs to see that Hugo's room was empty. The nurse told me he just died. I was so sad because I could have held his hand as he departed from this life. I cried out to God, feeling so guilty and sad. God comforted me, saying that there is no condemnation because Hugo is resting in His loving arms forever.

> Trust in the LORD with all your heart
> and lean not on your own understanding;
> in all your ways submit to him, and he will
> make your paths straight. (Proverbs 3:5–6)

- Ms. Josephine's Testimony at the Nursing Home

I accidentally met Josephine while I was in the game room at the nursing home playing TV tennis with a resident when I overheard an aide talking about her grandmother who was in a coma on the third floor. As I was listening, the Lord spoke to my heart and told me to go to her and introduce myself. I excused myself from the tennis game and introduced myself to the aide and explained to her that I worked with Calvary Christian Church in a nursing home ministry and I ministered and pray with patients. I then asked the aide if I could go upstairs and meet her grandmother. She said, "Yes, go on ahead, but she is in a coma and won't even know you are there." Of course, I disagreed with her in my heart.

When I arrived upstairs, she was resting while her two daughters were chatting. I introduced myself again and asked if I could pray with their mother. They affirmed and went downstairs for coffee. I stroked her face gently and prayed over her. I whispered in her ear all about Jesus Christ and how much He loved her and how He gave His life for her so that she could live with Him in peace forever. She started to stir, almost getting agitated, as she moved her head side to side on her pillow. Then she began to weep, saying she was a bad person and God hated her. I kept touching her face and telling her no, Jesus loved her. She kept saying, "No, no, no, I am a bad person." I told her He loved her just as she was and she just needed to ask Jesus to forgive her and He would be willing to forgive her right now and accept her as His beloved daughter. She cried harder and finally opened her eyes and asked Jesus to forgive her, and I told her He did. She was completely awake now and smiling as her two daughters returned to the room, and she told them that she loved Jesus Christ. I explained to her daughters what transpired, and they kept thanking me. Josephine was now asking for food because she was so hungry. The nurses came in with dinner, and they too were so shocked to see her sitting up, out of the coma, and as happy as could be. She just kept thanking Jesus, and everyone in her family visited her, and they were so thankful that she was alive. A few days later, however, she went home to be with Jesus. Two weeks later, while I was shopping in Salem, I bumped into her two daughters, and when they spotted me, they shouted and pointed my way, telling people in the line that I saved their mother. I immediately went to them and corrected them, telling them no, it was Jesus Christ Who saved their mother, and I was just a messenger for Jesus, a channel God used to bless their Mother. I assured them that they too can call upon His name and be saved, for anyone who calls upon the name of Jesus will be saved. Hallelujah!

That is my remarkable testimony of Ms. Josephine's salvation story.

Anyone who calls upon the Name of the
Lord will be saved. (Romans 10:13)

- Mr. Bill Testimony at the Nursing Home

I stopped at this Nursing Home because a woman from the women's home in Salem asked me to stop by and see her sister that worked there. Funny thing is, the elevator couldn't let me out because I did not have the code number. So when finally the elevator opened, I was in the basement where the kitchen and dining room were. Talk about God's perfect timing… As I walked into the dining room, a man began choking and was turning white, and people were shouting for a doctor. I began to shout the name of Jesus, Jesus, Jesus as I was running over to him, and as soon as I got there a bean flew out of his mouth, and he began to sneeze about ten times, and his color was restored. We gave God all the praise, glory, and honor. And that was how I met Mr. Bill. The woman I was going to meet there was one of the cooks in the kitchen, so I was able to meet her next and I introduced myself to her. That was a whole other testimony itself. I think the Lord allowed me to get stuck in the elevator so that I could meet Mr. Bill, who was almost choking to death. Again God's timing is perfect!

I then learned that Mr. Bill was transferred from a lock-down situation from another facility, and I began to befriend him and visit him on a weekly basis. One of the volunteers in the ministry I was coordinating knew him very well and was happy to take him to our church on Sundays, and she took him to dinner often. She even took him out to eat for his eightieth birthday. In fact, he gave his life to Jesus Christ on that special birthday, and he was so in peace, knowing that he would one day be with Jesus Christ forever. One day, while visiting him, we were reading God's Word together when he began singing and praising God. We loved to sing and praise God together after reading the Word, but this day was a little different. Before I came to visit Mr. Bill, God had put it on my heart in prayer that morning to bring a pad and pen with me, and I had no clue why. But I was determined to obey God when He told me something. After singing and praising God, Mr. Bill became very quiet, and he was getting depressed and forlorn. I asked him what was happening, and he asked me to pray for him so that he could repent of his sins and he wanted to tell me what they were. I agreed that he could trust me, and then he cried while he confessed his sins of violating his daughters when they were younger; they had not spoken to him for many years.

After he prayed and repented, he asked me if I would write his daughters a letter to tell them he was deeply sorry and also that he now had a relationship with God Who had forgiven him. In his letter, he asked them if they would forgive him of his wrongdoing and come to see him in the nursing home. He believed the pastor told him at his baptism that he was now set free from all his sins, guilt, and condemnation. He really needed to make it right with his girls, so here I was, equipped to write letters for him with the pen and paper God told me to bring with me that day. God is so amazing that sometimes I can only cry with the joy and love in my heart for Him. I wrote the letters, and he enclosed photos of himself from his recent baptism and signed and sealed them. I took them to the post office when I left. Mr. Bill now attends many Bible studies at the church on a weekly basis, and he is able to take "the ride" and attend many church events as well.

Another amazing thing happened that day when I left his room was that the director of the facility stopped me as I was leaving his room. She told me that he was an atheist and did not want anyone to talk to him about God. I told her that was not true because he had accepted Jesus Christ as his Lord and Savior and was now attending church services at our church. She said he was a recluse and never left his room, nor did he talk to anyone there at the nursing home. She was so amazed when I told her all that he was doing and how happy he was to call himself a Christian. She then asked me if I would consider having a church service at her facility so that many other residents could get set free as he had. She set a date and even asked if we could provide Communion before the residents had dinner. Service was set for 4:00 p.m. the next week. The service was successful with many of our volunteers present, and the function room was filled with about fifty residents all praising God and receiving Communion that day. Many other services were planned at that facility, and many gave their lives to Jesus.

The activities director asked me one day if I would do a weekly visit in the Alzheimer's unit at the facility as well. I told her I would pray about it, but she gave me one condition that I did not accept. She told me I could not mention the name of Jesus Christ since she was Jewish and there were many different religions in that facility that I must respect. I told her I could not comply to that since Jesus was my Lord and Savior Who brought me there to bless His people and to set the captives free. I told her how Jesus had set me free from addictions of alcohol and drugs and how He healed me, so I must honor Him and thank Him forever. God wants me to bring the Good News to everyone, and I must obey Him and not man. I did not accept her invitation; however, she called me the next week and said that it was okay that I spoke about my Lord Jesus Christ but that she would sit in on my appointment in the Alzheimer's unit. Of course, I accepted and approved.

This is how the appointment began…

I walked in to the large room of about fifteen patients who were all sitting around a large table, and most of them were half asleep and nonverbal. I quickly asked the Lord what I should do as I was feeling a bit unsure how to get their attention. He then told me to go to each one of them and hold their hand or touch their shoulder and sing "JESUS LOVES YOU" to them. I began with a woman at the head of the table and sang the song to her, and she began to cry, saying her mother sang that to her as a small child. She came to attention and cried and then smiled and began to help me to sing to the next person, who also came to life with tears running down his cheeks. I sang this song to each one of the patients around the table, until each person was alive, and we all sang the song together. At that point, when I had the attention of all fifteen people, I told them the story of the Little Teacup.

The Teacup Story

There was a couple who used to go to England to shop in the beautiful stores. They both liked antiques and pottery and especially teacups. This was their twenty-fifth wedding anniversary.

One day, in this beautiful shop, they saw a beautiful cup. They said, "May we see that? We've never seen one quite so beautiful."

As the lady handed it to them, suddenly the cup spoke.

"You don't understand," it said. "I haven't always been a teacup. There was a time when I was red and I was clay. My master took me and rolled me and patted me over and over, and I yelled out, 'Let me alone,' but he only smiled, 'Not yet.'"

"Then I was placed on a spinning wheel," the cup said. "And suddenly I was spun around and around and around. 'Stop it! I'm getting dizzy!' I screamed. But the master only nodded and said, 'Not yet.'"

"Then he put me in the oven. I never felt such heat!" the teacup said. "I wondered why he wanted to burn me, and I yelled and knocked at the door. I could see him through the opening, and I could read his lips as He shook his head, 'Not yet.'"

"Finally the door opened, he put me on the shelf, and I began to cool. 'There, that's better,' I said.

"And he brushed and painted me all over. The fumes were horrible. I thought I would gag. 'Stop it, stop it!' I cried. He only nodded, 'Not yet.'

"Then suddenly he put me back into the oven, not like the first one. This was twice as hot, and I knew I would suffocate. I begged. I pleaded. I screamed. I cried. All the time I could see him through the opening, nodding his head saying, 'Not yet.'

"Then I knew there wasn't any hope. I would never make it. I was ready to give up. But the door opened, and he took me out and placed me on the shelf.

"One hour later, he handed me a mirror and said, 'Look at you.' And I did. I said, 'That's not me, that couldn't be me. It's beautiful. I'm beautiful.'

"'I want you to remember, then,' he said, 'I know it hurts to be rolled and patted, but if I had left you alone, you'd have dried up.

"'I know it made you dizzy to spin around on the wheel, but if I had stopped, you would have crumbled.

"'I knew it hurt and was hot and disagreeable in the oven, but if I hadn't put you there, you would have cracked.'"

Lesson from the teacup story—this teacup story illustrates what Jeremiah wrote by the inspiration of God:

> The word which came to Jeremiah from the Lord saying, "Arise and go down to the potter's house, and there I shall announce My words to you." Then I went down to the potter's house, and there he was, making something on the wheel. But the vessel that he was making of clay was spoiled in the hand of the potter; so he remade it into another vessel, as it pleased the potter to make. Then the word of the Lord came to me saying, "Can I not, O house of Israel, deal with you as this potter does?" declares the Lord. "Behold, like the clay in the potter's hand, so are you in my hand, O house of Israel." (Jeremiah 18:1–6)

Moral of the Teacup Story

God knows what He's doing (for all of us). He is the Potter, and we are His clay. He will mold us and make us so that we may be made into a flawless piece of work to fulfill His good, pleasing, and perfect will.

May the teacup story become our story as we willingly yield to our Potter's hand. "I know the fumes were bad when I brushed and painted you all over, but if I hadn't done that, you never would have hardened, you would not have had any color in your life. And if I hadn't put you back in that second oven, you wouldn't survive for very long because the hardness would not have held."

Everyone loved the tea cup story as I portrayed it with real teacups, clay, and a spinning wheel. They enjoyed it so much that every week thereafter, they asked me to tell them this story. And the director told me after the first week that they would never remember it, and she was shocked to see the results of God's handiwork and the life it brought to these patients.

My heart is confident in you, O God, no
wonder I can sing your praises! (Psalm 57:7)

• Ms. Helen's Testimony at the Nursing Home

There were great "God moments" at this nursing facility today with my sweet friend Ms. Helen and her friends. I worked with her daughter at NSES, and one day she was telling me how sad she was because her mother was in a facility and how she had no choice because her dad recently passed away and she worked a full-time job. I asked her if she would give me permission to visit her mom since that was my ministry at CCC, and she accepted with joy. I met Ms. Helen and loved her immediately because she reminded me of my mom who had recently passed away. And she truly treated me like a daughter as well. She shared her life story with me being a teacher and a music leader at her church for over forty years. Because I too had been a kindergarten teacher, and I also had worked in the music ministry at church, we got along famously. We both had hearts for Jesus and for praising and worshipping God as well as loving children and bringing them to Jesus. When I first met her though, she was very sad and depressed, missing her husband and her life in her own hometown. I missed my mother too, so we connected quickly as we loved on each other. We quickly became dear friends. I visited her often, and we loved praising God, and before you knew it, she was no longer depressed. At first, she couldn't eat on her own, so I fed her and helped her become more independent. Soon she was able to feed herself and get around in a wheelchair. I took her outdoors to smell the fresh air. The herb garden was her delight, and sitting to hear the birds singing was another favorite of hers. She soon started taking sightseeing tours with other residents on the bus to the beach and around the North Shore. She was coming alive more than ever. Her daughter told me that Ms. Helen's birthday was approaching, so her daughter planned a birthday party for her and invited her friends and family from her hometown. I made her an awesome birthday cake with little children on it to recall the days when she was a teacher. The facility planned a wonderful dinner in the dining room, and Ms. Helen was overjoyed to see her family and friends.

We also met in the parlor of the facility often and sang songs with all the other residents, and that thrilled her beyond words. She was actually beginning to walk with the walker and did not need to be wheeled in the wheelchair.

She loved the Lord, and our time together met our spiritual needs with prayer, praise, and Bible study. One day in late

November, I asked her if she wanted to assist me at the piano so we could entertain the other residents. She was excited, and we played the piano together and sang songs for two hours. The interesting note is that I do not play the piano, but she was playing and teaching me as we were singing together, realizing that we were a great team. The other residents joined us as we sang and praised God, and the residents were shocked to hear her play and sing like an angel. After we worshipped God, we asked other residents if they too wanted to invite Jesus Christ into their hearts, and some accepted the invitation. Even the staff enjoyed our time, and some were filled with tears of joy watching her progress. I asked her if she would be willing to put on a Christmas concert to celebrate her daughter's birthday on December 5, and she agreed to do that; it would be her surprise gift to her daughter. I agreed to come to the home every day so we could practice our concert, and the facility would plan the event with tea and deserts, and they agreed to keep the surprise from Ms. Helen's daughter. They even agreed to send out invitations to her friends and family.

December 5 was the day of the Christmas concert and her daughter's fifty-fourth birthday celebration! When she entered, she was so shocked to witness her mother all dressed up in her Sunday outfit walking for the first time to the piano to sing "Happy Birthday" to her daughter. We then sang Christmas carols and her favorite worship songs; the first one she sang was "Amazing Grace." And everyone present witnessed that miracle with tears of joy and thanksgiving; there was not a dry eye in the place. It was hard to believe that just one year ago, she was so depressed and had to be fed each meal, and now she was alive again, walking with a walker and able to feed herself. It was delightful to see her filled with such joy and peace. Our friendship was a blessing to the very end when God opened heaven's gates and escorted her home. I will remember Ms. Helen's love forever!

> Give thanks to the Lord and proclaim his greatness. Let the whole world know what he has done. Sing to him; yes, sing his praises. Tell everyone about his wonderful deeds. Exult in his holy name; rejoice, you who worship the Lord. Search for the Lord and for his strength; continually seek him. Remember the wonders he has performed, his miracles, and the rulings he has given, you children of his servant Abraham, you descendants of Jacob, his chosen ones. (Psalm 105:1–6)

Nursing Home Photos of Special Residents I Will Never Forget

Pictures of some special residents I will never forget

More Testimonies of God's Faithfulness

Gemma and I blessed & rejoicing

- God Moments from My Retreat with my Prayer Partner

I want to reflect on my retreat week with my dearest friend and mighty prayer partner. When I was searching for an inn or a hotel for this retreat, I was trusting God Who knows me more than anyone else. I trusted Him for the most perfect room because I had never been to Vermont. Gemma was going to stay with her parents who lived close by to where my hotel was. I had to go online, and I needed to trust God without seeing it first, which made me hesitant. But I trusted Him, and He blessed me with a beautiful gift of relaxation and comfort for this prayer retreat. To my utter amazement, it was a room with not only a great view of the mountains of Vermont, but the most beautifully decorated room I had ever seen. The bed had a soft cuddly comforter and sheets, a chair for reading, and a magnificent sauna, and hot tub room. And adjoining that room was a prayer room which was perfect for us when we got together for prayer and intercession. It was the best retreat ever for comfort, peace, and joy with my Father and my prayer partner.

We prayed and interceded for days on end for our families, our personal needs, the needs of our churches, our government, and our world. We prayed for our upcoming election as well, and our godly choice won, praise God. After praying for hours this one particular day, we decided to go out to get a breath of fresh air. As we were walking, something beautiful caught our gaze. We looked up into the sky, and we saw a perfectly shaped strong arm with a hand reaching out to another hand in a dark and gloomy cloud. We believe that God was showing us the dark evil of the world and that He was reaching out to us telling us not to worry; He was in control and that no weapon formed against us would prosper. We were so excited and praised God for His protection and guidance and that He was pleased that we were obeying His Word and praying no matter what the situation looked like. "Keep your eyes on Him, for He is the author and finisher of our faith, and He has the whole world in His hands"—it was the message He gave to us.

The next day, after our prayer and intercession, we walked down to Lake Champlain, and again, God showed us another cloud formation in the sky, and I took a picture of it. We saw a cloud shaped as a dove, and it was surrounded by perfectly shaped angels dancing around the dove. We believed that God's angels were surrounding God, and that He sent those angels around us to protect us and guide us. The next cloud formation appeared as we walked and prayed in the spirit for those God told us to pray for. The cloud appeared to be two hands with arms reaching out to each other. And that was our sign that God's hand reaches out to us and always holds us with His righteous right hand.

> Don't be afraid, for I am with you. Don't
> be discouraged, for I am your God. I will
> strengthen you and help you. I will hold you up
> with my victorious right hand. (Isaiah 41:10)

Another day on our retreat, I tried to make a dinner reservation for me and Gemma, but all the fine hotels and restaurants were at full capacity because it was parents-and-students college weekend. We finally prayed and walked into the last restaurant in town and asked God for His grace and an available table. The hostess said she was so sorry, but we needed a reservation. We kindly told her we did not have one, but we asked our Heavenly Father to open the door for us if that was at all possible. Suddenly, as she looked around the restaurant, she said, "Oh, here we are, we have a beautiful table for you both." We were so amazed and excited to see God bless us again with another "God moment." God answers the prayers of the righteous all the time. We laughed and thanked God for meeting our needs and filling us with the joy of the Lord again! We enjoyed a marvelous dinner as children of the King of Kings and Lord of Lords!

Then to confirm this entire week and its revelations, I got a card from Gemma at the end of that week, and on the front was a picture of two hands reaching out to each other like in the cloud we saw. God is so amazing and always sends us confirmations of His faithfulness!

I will always remember how God richly blessed us with a great retreat and healed me of the torn rotator cuff. Hallelujah!

I can really see how important it is to keep a journal so that I can remember all the great times when God has moved in my life. I recall Charles Stanley saying in one of my devotionals that when you acquire a record or a journal of God's consistent rewards for doing His will, it is like praying and interceding for His will to be done. Then and only then will you be able to recognize the wisdom of obedience. I just love to review all the mighty things He has done in my life so that I can give Him all the glory, praise, and honor that He deserves.

- Another Experience of God's Faithfulness When in Need!

We were invited to visit and support an agency in Boston, a mission that supports pregnancy choices and unwed mothers to save unborn children. We heard about it from our church, who supported them, and we were interested to support them as well. After the presentation, we all left in search for a restaurant for dinner. We were in Boston, and it was a Saturday night, so everyone doubted if we could find a place to eat, and yes, we were all hungry. We stopped at a few establishments, only to know that one needed a reservation, especially on a Saturday night. We kept walking, and we all were getting discouraged, cold, and having a diabetic condition., I was actually getting weaker and it was becoming a must that I have dinner. Finally, as we were approaching a very expensive and exclusive French restaurant, I suggested we go in, and I would ask them for a table. They laughed at me and followed me in. I went to the desk and asked the gentleman if he had an available table for ten people. He asked if we had a reservation, and of course, I said no. I then told him we were children of the King of Kings and that God told me we could have dinner there. Well, he looked surprised but told me he would check it out, and we waited patiently. He returned moments later and told us to follow him as they put tables together to accommodate us. Everyone was shocked but happy, and they could not believe that I got us a table. I reminded them that God is our King and we are children of the King, Who said we have not because we ask not. He told us in the Bible to say things be not as though they were, and that was exactly what I was doing. We enjoyed a wonderful dinner in an exclusive French restaurant, and everyone got blessed. We were even able to share Jesus Christ's faithfulness with the staff. We supported the unborn children, and God blessed us!

> As for me, I watch in hope for the Lord
> to help. I wait confidently for God my savior,
> and He will certainly hear me. (Micah 7:7)

- It's Those Little Things That God Does That Leaves Me Breathless!

I could write a book on just the little things that God does for me that leave me breathless. That is why I must write about how awesome He is all of the time! For example, my husband was leaving for a weeklong hunting trip, and just as he said good-bye and left the house, my desk in my prayer room broke down. I used this desk all day and night as I prayed and interceded. So I immediately cried out to my Lord and said, "Now what do I do, and whom can I call to fix it?"

Those words just came out of my mouth when the door opened and my husband said, "Oops, I forgot the English muffins in the refrigerator."

I thought, "Wow, my desk legs just broke off my desk."

Rather than be aggravated, he took off his coat and told me he would fix it. That God moment lasted all week while I worked at my desk. Every day I thanked God with belief of His awesome kindness and love. I still will not forget what might seem like a small blessing, because to me, it was a huge blessing never to be forgotten.

Every day God blesses me, and I can write a book on just the God moments I have with God. Whenever I cannot open a jar or a bottle because of the arthritic condition of my hands, I just call upon Jesus and ask him to open it, and He does immediately. When I lose something, I ask Him where it is, and He finds it. When I cannot think of a word, I cry out to him, and He gives me the word.

He is always with me. Whether it is in a dream or a vision, He speaks to me. He is my greatest friend that I have ever had, and I just love Him so much that I do not have words strong enough to describe how much I love HIM. He is in control of my life, and I am thankful to Him always.

> Your arm is endowed with power; your hand is strong, your right hand exalted. Righteousness and justice are the foundation of your throne; love and faithfulness go before you. Blessed are those who have learned to acclaim you, who walk in the light of your presence, LORD. They rejoice in your name all day long; they celebrate your righteousness. (Psalm 89:13–16)

• A Tragedy Turns into a Miracle

While on our winter vacation in sunny Florida, my husband and I planned to spend a day together, which was long overdue. We headed out to Siesta Keys Beach, which was about an hour or so away. When we finally arrived, to our dismay, we could not find one available parking space. We rode around the largest parking lot I had ever seen, only to be dismayed and discouraged with not one available parking space. After about thirty minutes, we decided to try another beach close by, and it was on our way home, so he agreed to try it. My husband was losing patience, so I prayed that perhaps this beach would work since it was not as popular as Siesta Keys. Off we went to Nokomis Beach, and as we were driving and searching their parking lots, nothing was available there either. I secretly cried out to my Lord, and suddenly, I saw a car pulling out, so I screamed, "There it is, pull over and grab it!"

Never stop praying. (1 Thessalonians 5:17)

Hallelujah! I was excited that God heard my prayers so that I could enjoy His beautiful creation! I was excited since I had not been to a beach in a couple of years, so yes, I was anxious to find a parking space. We pulled in. I was praising God, but he could care less because he was not a beach enthusiast. But God found us a spot on the beach, and we dropped off our chairs and ran to go in the water and cool off in that one-hundred-degree-hot day and tired from driving for almost two hours.

The waves looked ominous, so I asked Len to hold my hand. As we were going in the water, suddenly we were separated by this undertow that pulled me in and flipped me around and around so I didn't know what hit me. Then a lady grabbed my hand to lift me out of the water, and she helped me get my balance. I could not see as I yelled immediately for her to help me because I was covered with crushed seashells in my nose, ears, in my bathing suit, and my head was full of crushed shells as well. She said that I was bleeding from all the crushed rocks and shells that scraped my body. She helped to clean me off, but I was still yelling that I couldn't see because I lost my glasses.

Then she shouted, "Who wears their glasses in the ocean anyway?"

I said, "I didn't know there was an undertow. I just wanted to dunk in and get cooled off."

She then called people to help us find my glasses, telling them that they were $500 ones and I couldn't see so please help. The search was on, and believe it or not, she was a prayer warrior. She asked me if I knew Jesus and if I had faith to believe that God could find them.

"Of course!" I yelled to her. "I, too, am a prayer warrior."

So we and many others joined hands and asked God to find my glasses. The search went on, and we were all looking for my Ray-Ban glasses for an hour or so. She told me the glasses would show up near someone who didn't believe, and they would know the power of God. We both agreed that it would strengthen someone's faith who really didn't believe in our miracle-working God.

> For I hold you by your right hand—I, the LORD your God. And I say to you "Don't be afraid. I am here to help you." (Isaiah 41:13)

She had to leave to do an errand and would return in an hour. So I and my husband decided to go and sit down since we had been looking for my glasses for over an hour, and he said they were lost forever in this horrific current. She left, and we walked back to our chairs to rest. I took a nap since I could not see in this bright sunshine without my transition glasses.

I woke up about forty-five minutes later, and I asked my husband to take me for a walk at the other end of the beach so I could look there for my glasses. He said it was impossible because of the strong current, but he agreed anyway. We stopped to talk to a couple who also lost something, and we shared my story with them. They wished us luck, and as we turned to walk away, Len looked down and said, "There are your Ray-Ban glasses!"

We picked them up, and sure enough, they were my glasses found at the other end of the beach. I began running back to where I fell in the water looking for my rescuer to share the good news! When I found her, I yelled, "God found my glasses." And everyone was yelling and screaming and giving God all the glory honor and praise. Of course, Doubting Thomas thought it was insane to find them in that violent tide. Hallelujah, and everyone on the beach praised God. Thank You, God, for Your faithfulness and Your mighty power as you blessed me again!

Thank You too for a new friend who is a prayer warrior and intercessor and who is a bold disciple of Jesus Christ.

> I wait quietly before God, for my victory comes from him. He alone is my rock and my salvation, my fortress where I will never be shaken. (Psalm 62:1–2)

> Those who are righteous will be long remembered. They do not fear bad news; they confidently trust the LORD to care for them. (Psalm 112:7)

• Tests Bring Testimonies, i.e., Rotator Cuff Tear

Then another test came, and you don't realize it will be a testimony at the time. You just pray, obey, and then He shows you His mighty power! I was in a golf tournament in Beverly, and I was so nervous that day. When I went to hit the ball on the first tee, I hit the ground with so much power that I tore my rotator cuff. Of course, I didn't know what I did until I saw the doctor later that week. I just couldn't move my arm, but due to my pride, I played all nine holes in pain and suffering. My golf days were short-lived, and I was preparing for upcoming surgery. My husband put away my golf clubs and hung my bike up in the shed because we knew I would be recovering for months according to the doctor. But God is so faithful and amazing… About two weeks before the surgery date, the nurse in charge at the hospital called me to prepare me for surgery, and she asked me to close my eyes and she would pray for me over the phone. Well, I was so delighted that the nurse could be a Christian and that she was going to pray for me. But as she began to pray, I realized that she was hypnotizing me, not praying. If you recall, I was familiar with the sounds from a hypnotist versus prayers from my God since I had worked for one. I immediately stopped her and said, "No thank you, I have a God that can heal me, and His name is Jehovah Rapha. I will ask Him to heal me, thank you."

When I hung up, I immediately felt heat flow all over my body like hot oil, and I knelt down and prayed to God for His healing power to fill me and heal my shoulder. After the prayer, my arm and shoulder were completely healed, and I could raise my arm up to the ceiling and move it every which way. I cried with joy and thanksgiving to my faithful God, thanking Him for discernment and faith. I went out to the shed and took my bike off the hook, and I went for a twenty-mile bike ride and have been healed ever since. The surgery was canceled. But that wasn't the only time I tore my rotator cuff either. I tore it again at the gym a few years later, and that too was healed after prayer, faith, and some physical therapy and exercise. Hallelujah!

• Testimony at the Hairdressers

I met a new hairdresser today, and as she was beginning to cut my hair, I thought she looked familiar. As she talked, even her voice was familiar. When she told me her name, a knifelike pain entered my heart, and I probably looked shocked! I then asked if she knew a man with that same last name.

She said, "Yes, it is my dad."

I wanted to vomit when she told me who her dad was; this man deceived me with alcohol and stole my youth at a very young age. I needed to go home and be with God to ask Him why I was there and what I should do. I had to get out of that place soon, but then I immediately had to change the subject until she finished cutting my hair. I left to seek God with this news. In fact, whenever I hear that song, it brings back bad memories I chose to forget so many years ago, and I get sick to my stomach. To this very day, I turn off the radio when I do. That evening, God had me feel the feelings, repent of my sins, and forgive this man who stole my virginity and broke my spirit.

I later found out that he suffered from cancer and was in a nursing facility with Alzheimer's disease at the early age of sixty-three. And God comforted me with this scripture.

> Dear friends, never take revenge. Leave that to the righteous anger of God. For the Scriptures say, "I will take revenge; I will pay them back," says the LORD. (Romans 12:19)

Visions/Dreams from God

- A Vision for a Friend

I had a dream, and there was food like stale bread, nuts, and cereal all over the lawn for the birds to feast on. All kinds of birds, hawks, and seagulls were in their glory. Then a large sparrow came along and knocked a small bird's nest out of the tree, and a baby sparrow lay injured. Birds were pushing the baby out of the way of their food and further injured the poor baby sparrow. One crow came along and tried to put a large piece of crust into the baby sparrow's mouth. Suddenly, God appeared on the scene and picked up the baby sparrow and held it in His hands, stroking the bird gently. God spoke quietly to the sparrow, saying to rest and trust Him and He would care for it.

"I will never leave you or forsake you," He said. "Be still and know that I am your God, and I will care for you forevermore. I will lead you and guide you, and I will always meet your needs only trust ME," says God. John 10:28 says, "No one will ever snatch you out of My hands."

God then began to feed the sparrow with an eye dropper one drop at a time. He rebuked the crows and the seagulls, saying she must only drink milk now, for it would choke her and kill her to eat bread that it could not even swallow. She must be nurtured and cared for and taught how to eat the bread of life. It was a sharp sword, and it could kill her if she was not ready for it.

Moral of dream—baby Christians must beware of the bullies who want to kill, steal, and destroy the little children. My friend was spared from the bullies who were tormenting her.

> I came to bring them life everlasting and
> love that will nurture and restore them back
> to me says God. (John 10:10)

• A Vision/Dream of My Best Friend

Angie and I were best friends back in the 1980s, and one night I had a dream that Angie was choking to death in her sleep while her husband was hunting in New Hampshire. In the vision, she was asleep and began choking on her own saliva. Her daughter who was in another room finally heard her in distress and ran to her mother to perform lifesaving procedures but was unsuccessful, and Angie passed away. This dream tormented me for a couple of weeks as I prayed asking God what I should do about this dream. After much prayer and intercession, God told me to visit Angie and to share Jesus Christ with her. I called her, and she invited me to her real estate office that she owned in her hometown. We had a lovely conversation about Jesus Christ, and I shared with her how much God loved her and wanted her to accept Jesus as her Lord and Savior, repent of her sins, and be His child forever. She was so excited that day, and as we prayed together, Angie had so much joy that she could not stop thanking me with the excitement that filled her heart. When I left her office, I remember how she opened her window, and from her second floor, she yelled down to me as I was walking to my car, "Carol, I love you so much, and thank you for giving me Jesus!" I can still see her laughing and crying at the same time so full of joy and peace.

The bittersweet ending to this story is that she died exactly like the vision I had two weeks prior to that day of her salvation. I will love and remember my dear friend, and I look forward to one day seeing her in heaven. Everyone who calls on the name of the Lord will be saved. (Romans 10:13)

- Another God Moment at the Beach

Why does the beach put a smile on my face and a joy in my heart? I can't pinpoint exactly why it does. Is it the sound of the waves and the screeching of the seagulls flying all around? Is it the warmth of the sunshine on my face? Or the cool balmy breeze that fills my heart with peace? Whatever it is, those are the sounds that soothe my soul and calm my mind. There is a freedom I get at the beach, looking at the blue sky and feeling the sunshine warm my heart. The salt water feels like medicine to my body, and the breezes clear my brain of the stress that so easily entangles me. I seem to sleep better at the end of a beach day, and all my worries vanish.

Yes, I love the beach! Now as I sit and relax from a hard day's work and open my Bible to enjoy my perfect day at the beach, a lady came and put her chair right next to mine.

I wanted to say, "What, with a six-mile beach to find a seat, you choose to sit right next to me?" But I quickly repented to God for that negative and selfish thought. The lady immediately introduced herself and began to tell me that she was sad and lonesome because her husband was ill and at the hospital preparing for heart surgery. I felt her pain and sadness as I introduced myself to her and told her I was Christian and that I ministered in hospitals and nursing homes. I then asked what I could do for her or how I could help relieve her pain. No, she just needed an ear and a shoulder to cry on as she shared her sadness and fear. I asked if I could pray for her and her husband, and she agreed. We joined hands, and I prayed for his upcoming surgery the next day, and I asked God to fill her heart with

His peace that passes all understanding. With tears in her eyes, we then prayed for her salvation as she accepted Jesus Christ as her Lord and Savior. Before she left the beach, we prayed in agreement that the Lord would save and heal her husband. Hallelujah, what a blessing to minister to His hurting children!

And that was my day at the beach ministering to a child of God for salvation, healing, and peace.

> All praise to God, the Father of our Lord Jesus Christ. God is our merciful Father and the source of all comfort. He comforts us in all our troubles so that we can comfort others. When they are troubled, we will be able to give them the same comfort God has given us. For the more we suffer for Christ, the more God will shower us with his comfort through Christ. Even when we are weighed down with troubles, it is for your comfort and salvation! For when we ourselves are comforted, we will certainly comfort you. Then you can patiently endure the same things we suffer. We are confident that as you share in our sufferings, you will also share in the comfort God gives us. (1 Corinthians 1:3–7)

Why I love the beach

The Home Addition and My Healing Journey

Part 1
Mold Detected Causes Health Problems

I smelled mold in the house and complained to my husband on several occasions but with no response. I then pursued the mold issue with God in prayer as I was worried about our health should mold be detected. Then the kitchen flooring was making a squishing sound like there could be water under the laminate floor. That led to some water beginning to seep through the cracks on the floor panels. I could smell the mold now, but I did not know where the water was coming from or if there was a leak somewhere in the house. I called a roofer to investigate for any leaks on the roof or in the attic, but nothing was found. Then a company who investigates and tests for mold was called in. He confirmed the mold in many of the rooms. I knew there was a leak, but where was it coming from?

One day while I was praying and asking God for His wisdom, He gave me a word in Isaiah 30:21 "Whether you turn to the right or to the left, your ears will hear a voice behind you saying, 'This is the way, walk in it.'" So I got up from my chair and began walking toward the kitchen when I heard the Lord's voice say, "Stop, there is the leak." I called my husband and asked him to remove the panel that covered the oil burner in the kitchen; sure enough there was the slow leak from the pipe that comes in from outdoors. We immediately called the Town of Danvers who came over, and they confirmed that there was a leak coming from the water hydrant outside our house. Immediately contractors from the city were called in to confirm that water was indeed under the floors and walls in the kitchen and the master bedroom that was located behind the kitchen. They found the mold, and I was asked to pack my bags and leave the house. I went to a nearby motel where I lived for over a month until all mold was eradicated. Now it was recommended to call a contractor to redo the kitchen; we then decided to add the addition to the house. My prayer to God is being fulfilled with a peace that surpasses all understanding, and His Word to extend my borders was now coming to pass! Hallelujah!

Part 2
Reason for the Addition to Our House

Adding an addition to our home had been my dream and prayer since we were married. However, now my prayers were answered because of the mold. It was imperative to remove the mold, and it was an opportunity to add on an addition to the house. I had issues with my washing machine being in the kitchen and the dryer was outside in the garage. Furthermore, there was never any space for our grandchildren to have a sleepover so we could enjoy them for any length of time. That always grieved me.

So now due to the mold issue, we are shopping for an architectural contractor to draw up the plans and a general contractor to do the makeover. We decided on a master bedroom and en suite with an attached laundry room. We agreed on a huge playroom for guests to sleepover and a pool/ping-pong table for entertainment. We wanted to add a huge deck in the backyard with an above-ground swimming pool for the grandkids. We went to the bank and secured a bank loan, hired a contractor, and the work would begin in a week or so. Then all the machinery was delivered and parked on our property. That following week, the yard was dug up, a foundation was ready to be poured, and lumber was being delivered. Suddenly, I did not have a peace in my heart. When I told Len that, he told me that the bank had just sent us a letter and rejected the home loan. I was mortified because they had already dug the hole in the ground and now we would not have the down payment to begin the job.

My heart was grieved; so my next step was to seek God for His wisdom. I repented for having them dig the hole with no money in hand to make the deposit for this job. I told God that we would never have let the contractors dig the hole had we known earlier of the bank's refusal. I went to the river to seek the Lord as I had to cast all my cares on Him and pray for His wisdom. I began to walk, pray, and praise God for His peace that passes all understanding. I was praying in the spirit as I walked around the track several times when my cell phone rang. It was my cousin Richie, so I answered and immediately asked if his mom, who is my cousin, was okay because she had been sick. He responded, "Yes, she is okay, but you need to sit down, Aunty Carol, before I tell you why I am calling."

I found a bench near the baseball field, sat down, and said, "Okay, what is it, Richie, that you need to tell me?" He told me to recall the day he had asked me and Len to invest in his new business about six years ago. Yes, I told him that I remembered giving him $50,000. At the time I was not too happy about using our only savings to invest in his business. However, after we prayed, the Lord told us to invest. Well, he told me that he was now sending us a check for $60,000 this week with another check coming in the mail for $50,000 more. I immediately burst into tears, revealing to him our dilemma about the rejection from the bank for the house loan. The miracle was that $60,000 was the exact amount we needed as a down payment for the job. Richie then said that there would be another check coming to us soon for $200,000.00, which would cover the costs of our entire addition and all the furnishings to complete our new addition. I thanked Richie with tears and thanksgiving for God's miracle-working power. God answered my prayers over and above all I could possibly think or imagine. We gave our tithe to our church first of all, as I have always done in the past. This is the great testimony of my loving and faithful God who owns this earth and all that it contains. He blesses those who give, and I had just given my paycheck to my sister, who really needed money that week. God gave it back to me, pressed down, shaken together, and running over. In fact, He gave back more than I could think or imagine. God always confirms His Word to me, and I am so blessed, grateful, and thankful to my ever-faithful God!

> Give and you will receive. Your gift will return to you in full—pressed down, shaken together to make room for more, running over, and poured into your lap. The amount you give will determine the amount you get back. (Luke 6:38)

Part 3
First the Mold Then the Cancer Diagnosis

I was then diagnosed with cancer of the uterus and was scheduled for a complete hysterectomy at a major cancer hospital in Boston. I put the surgery off for about a month while I prayed and fasted for God's wisdom in this matter. I just wanted to believe God for my healing and not trust in man. But my husband and my family could not understand my wishes to believe God for a healing and insisted that I go for the surgery. I finally decided to trust God and submitted to the hysterectomy. While I was being prepped and surrounded by doctors and nurses, my blood pressure rose to almost three hundred. Fear and concern filled the room. No matter what they did, it would not drop. Finally I told them that I needed to pray and sing to my Lord. They said, "Go for it, Carol." I prayed aloud and then began singing "Amazing Grace." As I was finishing the song, my blood pressure dropped to normal, and they cheered and immediately wheeled me into the operating room. I do not recall another thing until I was in the recovery room and the doctor told me he was confident that he removed all the cancer. I thanked God for healing me, but I decided not to do chemotherapy and radiation. The recovery process was a long three months with no driving, no lifting, and with plenty of rest. I truly missed going to church on Sundays and going to the weekly prayer meetings. I truly missed the fellowship of my friends and coworkers at the job. I was getting desperate to go back to church and prayed for a miracle that soon I would be able to drive again. My prayer to you, O Lord…

> One thing I ask from the LORD, this only do I seek: that I may dwell in the house of the LORD all the days of my life, to gaze on the beauty of the LORD and to seek him in his temple. (Psalm 27:4)

Part 4
Len's Call from a Pastor at CBC

I had been recovering from surgery as I mentioned earlier and have not been going to church for about three months now while recuperating. One Saturday evening, Len got a telephone call from a patient, asking him to meet him at a church in Peabody before he preached his Sunday service. Well, that was all so new to me since Len never discussed his office or his patients with me. I asked him why he needed to go to a church to meet a pastor. That's when Len told me that this pastor was a patient who called and asked Len to adjust him before he preached that Sunday. I was shocked and said, "I haven't been to church in three months, and I want to come with you." He said not to expect him to stay for the service, but he would wait in the car. I said, "What will it take for you to believe in God?"

He said, "Not until I see the holes in the hands of Jesus will I believe or become a born-again Christian."

I replied, "I no longer care. Please just take me to church. I need to go to church!" I was now becoming desperate to go to the house of the Lord. When we arrived, Len met with the pastor, and after that, Len introduced me to him as he was about to walk into the sanctuary. Len said he would wait for me in the car, and the pastor asked, "Why aren't you going to stay for the service with your wife? Can't you just take an hour and join her and get blessed?"

Len half-heartedly agreed, and into the sanctuary we went. We all worshipped God, and then the pastor announced the title of his message: "Doubting Thomas." I started to cry and almost slid off the pew, remembering what Len had said to me the night before. The message was awesome, and at the end of the service, I ran up to the pastor with tears in my eyes as I told him how blessed I was and about the Doubting Thomas conversation Len and I had the night before. He then asked Len if he was willing to make a commitment for six weeks to listen to this message series of "Doubting Thomas." Len reluctantly agreed.

To my amazement we went to church for six weeks, and I actually fell in love with the church, the people, and the pastors. By April, we were still there at Calvary Baptist Church, a.k.a. CBC. I consulted with my pastor at Calvary Christian Church, a.k.a. CCC, whether I should leave there and go to CBC with Len since now he is considering baptism. My pastor agreed and told me I should be with my husband at the Baptist Church and that they will always be praying for us. As sad as I was, I needed to obey God and submit to my husband, Len. He was soon to be baptized. Hallelujah!

Part 5
Len's Baptism at CBC

The great day came after almost twenty years of prayer. Len will finally give his life to Jesus Christ. I remember there was a song that he heard while watching a movie that touched his heart and moved him to tears. The song was "Mary Did You Know" by CeeLo Green. He even got the CD and played it constantly.

The pastor was counseling Len before the day that he would be baptized, but Len did not want to write his testimony nor was he willing to share it before the church. But with much prayer and intercession, Len finally agreed, and the date was set for the baptism at Calvary Baptist Church.

Many of our good friends, family, and my prayer partners were invited to this upcoming and blessed event. Present were our new friends from CBC, some of my old friends from CCC, my children and grandchildren, my sister and her family, Len's family, and many of my prayer partners who had been praying for Len for many years. God's anointing that day was incredible, especially when he publicly repented of his sins to God and to the church; there was not a dry eye in the building. We watched with tears in our eyes as Len was dunked in the baptismal tank and he came up as a new man in Christ. That was the day he accepted Jesus Christ as his Lord and Savior and God removed the scales from Len's eyes. He could finally see God and weep with repentance for his sins publicly while the onlookers cheered with praise and thanksgiving to our mighty God.

Another great blessing came weeks later when Len's daughter and her family accepted Jesus Christ as their Lord and Savior and were baptized. Following that blessing, my sister and her family gave their lives to Jesus. Then my dear friend Jeannie, whom I've loved and shared the Lord with for over thirty years, accepted Jesus and invited us to her baptism at Calvary Christian Church. She told Len that it was because of his testimony that God touched her heart after many years of rebellion; now she was ready to commit her life to God. We were filled with joy to finally witness her baptism. She became involved at CCC and joined the music ministry, writing her own songs as well as playing the guitar. The blessings we all enjoyed from Len's baptism were amazing.

The sad news came when Jeannie passed away with cancer two years later. But I am thankful to God that she accepted Jesus Christ as her Lord and Savior and she is now in heaven for all eternity.

Part 6
My Sister Dies of Leukemia and My
Mother Dies of a Broken Heart

Sister dies then my Mother dies 3 months later after her 90th birthday

I had just lost my sister with leukemia, having suffered for six months with chemotherapy and radiation. I watched her suffer beyond belief, along with the pain and suffering of her two children and her family to lose such a beautiful human being. That same pain and suffering caused my mother to suffer as she watched her firstborn child die, and that was horrendous. She wanted God to take her, not her daughter. But God's ways are not our ways, I'm sad to say. Then I found out that my dear friend was in the room next to my sister's at hospice, and he too died the same day. I could not even attend his services. Three months later, I watched my mother suffer with a broken heart, and she died at the same hospice facility. I stayed with my mother every day and night for a week until that last day when she opened her eyes to thank me and tell me she loved me. She closed her eyes with a smile on her face and went home to heaven with Jesus. Then I learned that another good friend of mine died of cancer and was being waked that evening at the same funeral home as my mom. Now my body was tired, forlorn, and weary. This was the time I had to take a vacation from the nursing home ministry at CCC as I needed time to heal from stress and the great losses in my life. I needed to seek God's face for His peace and love to envelope me at this grievous time in my life. God speaks to me in the night to bring peace to my heart.

> The righteous cry out, and the Lord hears them; He delivers them from all their troubles. (Psalm 34:17)

> Wait for the Lord; be strong and take heart and wait for the Lord. (Psalm 27:14)

Part 7
The Cancer Returns

The following year during my checkup at Dana Farber, I was diagnosed with metastatic cancer that spread to my bones, cervical cuff, and lungs. The doctor scheduled me for an appointment to discuss chemotherapy and radiation, which I was determined never to consent to after seeing my sister and many of my dear friends and family suffer and die. I desperately prayed to God for another healing!

I told my family that I would go to the appointment to appease them. I called my prayer partner and friend to come with me to the chemotherapy appointment for support and prayer. While the nurse was examining me, I had a horrific nonstop fit of coughing while lying on her examining table. The nurse stopped the examination and told me to see my doctor for an antibiotic before she could further discuss chemotherapy with me.

My friend and I left the hospital, walked to my car in the parking garage, and prayed to God for His wisdom. We believed that the Lord did not want me to schedule any further chemotherapy appointments. We drove away, and I never coughed again after that incident. I felt as though the devil was confusing me, but I knew that God is not a God of confusion, and I stood my ground in faith, believing my God who said I was healed in Jesus's name. (1 Peter 2:24).

A couple weeks later, the hospital called and scheduled an appointment for me to see a radiologist to discuss radiation therapy. So now my friend and I headed to Boston again. When we got to the radiation department, I signed in, and we were escorted to the waiting room. I was grieved when I saw the people coming from their treatment; they were all so tired, weak, and pale. The odor was so horrendous like burnt flesh and it nauseated me. About ten minutes later, the nurse came out to inform us that the radiation machine just broke, and we needed to reschedule the appointment for a later date. Again, we left the hospital asking God how a machine like that breaks down in a major cancer hospital.

We left Boston, and while driving home, we prayed to God for His perfect will for my life. I then decided *not to pursue* any treatment and I would stand on the Word of God and believe Him for my healing. And maybe, just maybe, I could become that miracle that the pastor was preaching about at church. No more confusion from the devil because God truly showed me that He was my great and mighty Physician. Jehovah Rapha is His name!

After that horrendous diagnosis, I signed myself out of the hospital's care and treatments; and I decided to trust God for my healing. I decided to live one day at a time, and I vowed to enjoy each day like it was the first day of the rest of my life. I chose not to be sad, fearful, or depressed. My plan was to love God with all my heart, soul, mind, and body and to trust Him for my life is in His hands. Not my will Lord, but Your will be done in me. I put my faith in God, and He became my strength, my hope, and my deliverer! And He always speaks to me through His Holy Word.

> I sought the Lord, and he answered me; he delivered me from all my fears. Those who look to him are radiant; their faces are never covered with shame. This poor man called, and the Lord heard him; he saved him out of all his troubles. The angel of the Lord encamps around those who fear him, and he delivers them. (Psalm 34:4–7)

I contacted many of my favorite pastors and preachers that I trusted and listened to and asked them for prayers of healing and deliverance.

Many sent me messages, books, and prayers to stand on for my healing. My prescription (Rx) from God was meditating, memorizing, and confessing His Word which became a daily necessity for me. I knew that I needed to eat the bread of life and drink the living water more than any food or drink the world could offer me. The more I fasted, studied, and meditated on His life-giving and sustaining Word, I fell deeper in love with Him and believed for my healing, in Jesus's name. I became more interested in the mighty men and women of the Bible who sinned and repented and how God forgave, healed, and delivered them of their sicknesses and diseases.

I especially loved the stories of King David and how God called him "the man after God's own heart." I too wanted to become a woman after God's own heart. One day I read in

Charles Stanley's devotional the following: "King David served God's purpose when he lived, and continues to do so hundreds of years later...every follower of Christ has been blessed by King David's obedience, service, and literary skill. He is a great example of what God can accomplish through us if we yield our life to Him." And that is what I wanted to do with my life. I wanted to love Him more and more with all of my heart, soul, mind, and body. I committed to yield my life to Him and stand upon His Holy Word forever! Hallelujah!

I listened to Pastor Prince teach on Communion and that became part of my prayer time every day. I started to receive Holy Communion every morning and I thanked God for each new day of life. I would remember all that He has done for me in the past and all He would do in the future with thanksgiving and praise. And before I went to bed each night, I would kneel before Him and humbly pray that if it be His perfect will for me to live, then I would be there in His presence in the morning for prayer, praise, and thanksgiving. Therefore, I received Holy Communion each day thereafter purposing in my heart to stay in His holy presence by praying, praising God, and interceding for the world. I attended prayer meetings and prayed for all who were suffering with sickness, infirmities, and afflictions.

God called me many years ago as His intercessor and to stand in the gap at the wall and pray for all His children to accept Jesus Christ as their Lord and Savior. Since I did not feel that I was called to go to the mission fields, I knew in my heart that my prayer room was my mission field. I committed to pray for all God's people, whenever and wherever He sent me. Every day I went into my prayer room, shut the door, entered into His presence with praise and thanksgiving. I confessed my sins and would ask God to shine His flashlight into my heart and show me anything that offended Him so I could repent. I am thankful that He is my Jehovah Rapha, the God who heals me. Like the pastor said in his message, why wait for a miracle? Be one. So that led me to pray and ask God, "How do I become that miracle?"

It has now been many years since that diagnosis, and I am still alive to tell the world about God's awesome miracle-working power to heal, to save, to forgive, and to set the captives free. Again, I believe that He allows the tests so that if we believe and embrace His promises, the testimony will come, and my God will get all the glory, honor, and praise.

> Taste and see that the Lord is good;
> blessed is the one who takes refuge in him.
> Fear the Lord, you his holy people, for those
> who fear him lack nothing. (Psalm 34:8–9)

Part 8
Another Challenging Testimony

Another challenging experience happened that was causing much suffering and dismay. My heart rhythm was out of control, and I was taken to a major hospital in Boston. I was scheduled for an electrical cardioversion which was another frightening experience for me. We were all in a ward being prepared for this procedure, several beds separated by curtains. The most frightening of all was when I saw the man in the bed across from me being zapped because the curtain was left open. When they zapped him, his body jumped about two feet in the air. Now I knew what to expect when it as my turn, and I prayed to God for peace and strength. However, when it was my turn, it did not work, and they had to zap me three times, and I had severe and painful burns on my chest and back. Two doctors were at the foot of my bed, and I heard them say that they were keeping me comfortable because I was suffering from metastatic cancer and I did not have much time to live. I heard what they said and I got upset; I sat up and I rebuked the doctors, telling them they had no right to confess that diagnosis on me. I said only God knows my time of arrival, not man. I left the hospital that night and never got paddled again. I will only believe God's report, not man's, in Jesus's name. I have since shared my testimony on a local television show, and I am about to finally publish my book to proclaim God's faithfulness and His power to save, to heal, and to deliver me in Jesus's name! Hallelujah!

> I will exalt you, LORD, for you rescued me. You refused to let my enemies triumph over me. O LORD my God, I cried to you for help, and you restored my health. You brought me up from the grave, O LORD. You kept me from falling into the pit of death. (Psalm 30:1–3)

Part 9
My Testimony at the Dentist

I had a terrible toothache on my bottom right side of my mouth during these trials with the cancer diagnosis. I saw my dentist, but I was not happy with the results, so my friend referred me to her dentist. I made an appointment for a second opinion and the doctor confirmed an infection and the need for immediate treatment. He referred me to a local surgeon, and I was scheduled to meet him the next day. I was disappointed when the surgeon advised me to surgically remove the tooth and have a bridge made at the outrageous cost of $23,000. I was mortified, so I went back to see my friend's dentist to share with him my dilemma. I told him of the diagnosis with metastatic cancer in my lungs, bones, and cervical cuff and that the doctors didn't give me much hope without the treatments they advised. But since I rejected the medical treatments, I still needed to take care of the infection immediately. I also told him that I signed myself out of the doctor's care in the Boston hospital and I decided to trust my God for my healing in Jesus's name. Therefore, I asked him if he could just clean out the infected tooth and put in a temporary tooth while I believe God for my healing. He was so sorry and he agreed to do that for me.

My tooth stopped aching with prayer and God's grace. God then asked me again whose report was I was going to believe: the doctors' or His. I told God that I decided to trust Him and believe Him to heal me or take me home because I was ready to meet my Maker! "Your will be done Lord, not mine" was my plea to God.

After a few weeks, my tooth stopped hurting and the infection was gone. I then asked the doctor to replace the temporary tooth with a permanent tooth because it was less costly. The good news is that today, many years later, my tooth is healed.

Every year I go for my dental checkups, I thank God for His miracle-working power and for my dentist who is always so kind and gracious to me, my husband, and all the patients we have referred to him.

And every year that I go to my primary care physician for my physicals, she too is so amazed and happy that I am healed and alive to share my story of God's amazing grace and love! I have since shared my testimonies with all the doctors who have treated me, and they too are amazed and blessed.

> I love the Lord because He hears my voice and my prayer for mercy. Death wrapped its ropes around me; the terrors of the grave overtook me. I saw only trouble and sorrow. Then I called on the Name of the Lord and He saved me. (Psalm 116:1)

Part 10
Len's Cancer Diagnosis and My Stroke Testimony

As you will see, the devil does not give up on me and I have learned to fight the good fight of faith and to trust in my God in every area of my life. I have learned to hold on to the hem of

Jesus's garment and the horns of His altar and to not give up my faith no matter what comes against me.

Len got diagnosed with lung and esophagus cancer, and God blessed him after lung surgery, with no chemotherapy treatments, just radiation on his esophagus. We were so thankful to God that he recovered. However...

Here is the story when I have a stroke and we are in the same hospital; he is recuperating from lung surgery and I am recovering from a stroke.

Here is my story of the stroke:

First, I must interject with my neighbor Nancy's story which is what led me to *the stroke*.

I have known Nancy and her family since I was five years old; we were next-door neighbors. When my mom took ill in 2006, Nancy helped me to care for my mom; she became my mother's dearest friend. She would take mom for walks or rides in her car in the evening to get a bite to eat or just go to the beach for an ice cream. I truly appreciated all she did to help me since my mom would not leave her home to live with any of her children. She definitely was not willing to go to a nursing facility. But caring for mom every day was wearing on me, and I prayed to God for some needed assistance.

One day, I scheduled an appointment with North Shore Elder Services for assistance. I met with the director and he was willing to help me with my mother. He offered me a job for twenty hours a week and he would send home health-care services to Mom on those days. This way, rather than spending all my time and energy cleaning Mom's house and doing her shopping, the agency would do those menial tasks so that I could spend quality time with my mother. I was thankful for this agreement and for the job to keep me involved with the agency which proved to be a blessing for the nursing home ministry. Nancy was also a blessing as she helped care for my mom when I was not available.

One night Nancy decided to take a walk to CVS, and as she was crossing County Street, she was hit by a pickup truck. She became hospitalized, but I had no idea where she was, and for days I tried to locate her. Due to the HIPPA laws, no one would tell me anything. I then began to search for her son, who was her health-care proxy, and that was a dead end as well. I finally called the Peabody Police Department to report her and her son missing. God made a way for me to get the police to finally give me information to their whereabouts. She was at Beverly Hospital due to the car accident, and he had a heart attack and was at Lahey Hospital in Burlington. Because there was no one to care for Nancy now, the state then admitted her to a nursing home facility. Therefore, she was no longer available to care for my mother either.

The police called to inform me that they found her son at Lahey Hospital suffering from a major heart attack. I was now able to get information from a nurse named Sammy who then gave me permission to visit him on Friday. When I prayed to God that morning I told Him I would go the next day, which was Saturday, to visit him. When do you tell God what to do when He told me specifically to visit Jeff on Friday? That was my mistake. So being a hot day, I went swimming in my pool and planned on a quiet restful day to end the summer. Suddenly, while floating on my raft, the pool began to spin, and I could not hold on to anything. I went to reach for the telephone which was on the steps, when the phone dropped into the pool and I fell off the raft, spinning around in fear. I realized then I could be dying perhaps of a heart attack since I was on a heart medication for a-fib. I cried out to Jesus to help me to get out of the pool so I wouldn't drown. By the grace of God, I managed to stop spinning and to get out of the pool and

I crawled into the house. I knelt at the couch and asked God to forgive me of my sins and to take me home if it be His will. God then told me to reach on the end table and use my cell phone and call 911. When a woman answered, I gave her my name and address, shouting that I could be having a heart attack. She could not hear a word I said, telling me it was a bad connection. I yelled louder my name, address, and phone number, but all I heard was: "I cannot hear you, I am sorry," and the call ended.

I then realized my time was up for sure. Within minutes the door burst open with firemen and EMTS who put me onto a stretcher. They examined me and proceeded to take me in the ambulance to a hospital. Traffic was horrendous, and they could not get me to a hospital in Burlington, Boston, or to Salem, so they had to take me to a local hospital. I was not happy, but I had no choice. Besides, Len worked across the street from that hospital, so at least he would be notified and would be there immediately. I was then diagnosed with an inner ear infection after taking X-rays and CT scans, and I was kept in the emergency room. I called the desk several times to get some food and told them I was a diabetic plus I needed to go to the bathroom, but I had no response. I became angry by 2:30 a.m. and I called Len to tell him I was walking out of this hospital and he had better pick me up. They never helped me even though I kept calling the nurses' station for assistance. After a few hours I walked to the desk with the tube in my arm to ask a nurse to remove it because I was leaving the hospital. The lack of care, help, or assistance when I called them several times infuriated me, especially when I saw the nurse at the desk playing solitaire on his computer while I had been buzzing for help for so long. I was relieved when Len arrived at 2:45 a.m. to take me home. Around 3:30 a.m., while resting in bed at home, the room began to spin again, and I started vomiting several times. We dressed immediately and Len took me to Lahey Hospital in

Burlington. I was in ICU diagnosed with a stroke and strapped to a bed after many tests and scans were performed. For a couple of days while in ICU, I kept hearing Jeffrey's name as the nurses talked to each other. I tried to get some information from them, but no one would answer me due to HIPPA laws. I prayed and finally remembered the nurse's name that I spoke to on the telephone that Friday when I was looking for Jeff. So I asked if Sammy could visit me when she came on duty. She finally came to see me and I asked if there was a Jeffrey in ICU.

I was thankful that Sammy remembered me and my telephone call when I was looking for him. She remembered me being a close neighbor with his family. She then agreed to let me visit Jeff because he was in room 2, which was directly next to mine. I was in room 1. That was the unbelievable miracle! The nurses strapped me onto a wheelchair and took me into Jeff's room because she said he did not have much time to live, and I had better see him now. When I saw him and reminded him of who I was, he opened his eyes and looked right at me. I began to tell him about Jesus Christ and how Jesus loved him. I told him if he called on Jesus Christ, He would take him home to heaven; I told him not to worry about his mom because I would take care of her. I knew that even in a coma, he could hear me, and I encouraged him as I spoke words of love and peace to him. "Just call on Jesus, and He will take you home, Jeff." He looked relieved when he turned his head to face me, only now with closed eyes. I had been telling him to give his life to Jesus for many years, but today I told him was his day of salvation. After I prayed for Jeff, I was taken back to my room. Later I learned that Jeff went home to Jesus.

I realized then why I was taken to that hospital and no other...that I was supposed to have gone to see Jeffrey on Friday, and not go swimming in my pool. The confirmation came when the phlebotomist entered my room later that day to draw blood samples. He looked so familiar and I realized that he was the same man that I met four years ago at Lahey when I had the a-fib diagnosis. I was so shocked when he asked me the same question he asked back then: "Are you a Christian, and do you know Jesus Christ?"

"Of course," I said as I had a Bible lying across my chest. I could not read it because I had wires and tubes running in both arms, but at least His Word was on my heart. Then I realized he was the same man from years ago who at the time I thought was an angel. He asked if he could read the book of Jonah to me. Again I said yes because he did read it to me before. I commented that I must not have understood God's message to me back then, and why does God want me to read it again? Of course, now I know after recovering and hearing what God was trying to teach me back then. I disobeyed God when he told me to go to see Jeff that Friday morning, but instead I chose to go swimming in the pool on that hot day. That's when I told God I would visit him on Saturday since Len was going to close the pool. I read it again and again, prayed over and over for God to confirm to me why I was in this hospital again a few years later with the same phlebotomist telling me the same story of Jonah. I think by now I understand the book of Jonah and how important it is to obey God when He tells you to do something. Obedience is faith's foundation. I was selfish and wanted one more day in the pool rather than obey God and go to visit Jeff on Friday when God told me to. The price we must pay when and if we disobey God who loves us and wants the very best for His children. This was a devastating time for me with Len down the hall recovering from cancer surgery and I was now recovering from a stroke. However, God did minister to me during that time, allowing me the gift of repentance and then to share my testimony with other patients along with the staff that treated me. God's grace is so amazing!

The American flag dedicated to Jeff for his service was
presented to me for his mom in the nursing home.

Wait for the LORD; be strong and take
heart and wait for the LORD. (Psalm 27:14)

"And we know that God causes everything to work together for the good of those
who love God and are called according to His
purpose for them."(Romans 8:28)

Part 11
My Next Journey to Rehabilitation

Four weeks later, I was sent to a rehabilitation center via
ambulance to continue to heal. I left Len at Lahey, and that concerned me for sure. After I was put into my new room, which
was beautiful, the nurse told me I had to see a psychiatrist the
next morning at 7:00 a.m. I panicked at first and could not sleep
because I thought the doctor heard about all my witnessing to the
staff at the hospital. I became frightened and cried out to God as
I read the Bible and prayed all that night. When the psychiatrist
came into my room the next morning, he asked me why I was

brought to that facility. I just could not believe how God gave me the words to say, and I told him my entire life story, including my salvation, my ministry, and the testimonies of my Lord. He listened patiently as I was filled with the peace of God that passes all understanding. I told him my story, and he believed it. He said he wanted me to go home and finish my book because he believed my story and why God allowed the stroke to happen to me. He said may God's will be done in my life. He believed the entire Jonah story and the visitations from the phlebotomist. He wished me well and said I must give him a copy of my book when it is published. I promised him that I would. The doctor discharged me the next day, and I vowed to my Lord that I would continue to meditate on His Word day and night and continue to write my book to glorify and honor *Him* for God reassured me that final day at the rehabilitation hospital these words from His Holy Bible:

> I will not die but live, and I will proclaim
> what the LORD has done. (Psalm 118:17)

Part 12
Eye Testimony

During my routine eye examination, my doctor told me that my eye is hemorrhaging and I would need to make an appointment with a retina specialist. Another obstacle I must overcome. After that diagnosis it was prescribed that I get injections into my eyeballs to stop the bleeding. That was frightening news for me that I almost could not go through with it. With weeks of prayer and intercession, I believed God was telling me to fight the fear and that He would be with me as my Mighty Warrior and to be still and submit. Well, I finally obeyed God and submitted to this treatment. My optometrist, who is a Christian friend as well, agreed to come with me to my first appointment and agreed to pray with me and for me. My choice was to get the injections or go blind, and that was another challenge for me to trust God. With many tears and prayers, I finally began the treatments, and within six months of injections, the bleeding subsided. Best of all, I no longer had fear. I was delivered from the fear of man and the enemy who is always trying to kill me and destroy my faith in God. I thank God every day for His presence and His love and mostly for delivering me from fear. I rejoice for this healing miracle for my eyes and for my body, in Jesus's name.

I love you, LORD, my strength.

> The LORD is my rock, my fortress and my deliverer; my God is my rock, in whom I take refuge, my shield and the horn of my salvation, my stronghold.
>
> I called to the LORD, who is worthy of praise, and I have been saved from my enemies. (Psalm 18:1–3)

I cannot explain why I have had so many interruptions and hindrances to writing this book. I ask myself if perhaps these incidents or tests in my life had to happen so I could have the testimonies to write the book. So I believe that the test comes before the testimony. I have learned that God allows these trials and tribulations to teach us, perfect us, and equip us for His transforming work in us. He tells us that no sin or sickness, nor deceit or darkness, will be able to enter heaven. Therefore, I will be transformed into His image and likeness so that I can proclaim to the world how He has *rescued* me, healed me, and set me free.

> The righteous person may have many troubles, but the LORD delivers him from them all; He protects all his bones, not one of them will be broken. (Psalm 34:19–20)

The Lord will rescue me from every evil attack and will bring me safely to His heavenly kingdom. (2 Timothy 4:18)

I will exalt you, LORD, for you rescued me. You refused to let my enemies triumph over me. O LORD my God, I cried to you for help, and you restored my health. You brought me up from the grave, O LORD. You kept me from falling into the pit of death. (Psalm 30:1–3)

Christ's presence and His Word has always offered me comfort, strength, and motivation to persevere with tenacity and faith. I will always remember Him intervening for me in my life as He continues to hold my hand with His righteous right hand. He promised me that He will never leave me or abandon me. That strength is always available to me with an abundance of peace, joy, and love.

Praise our faithful and awesome God!

How much more do I need to say? It would take too long to recount the many stories of the faith and the testimonies I have witnessed in my body personally and at nursing facilities and at many hospitals. We have all placed our hope in a better life with Jesus Christ. Hallelujah! For God told me in the book of James 1:12, that blessed is the one who perseveres under trial because having stood the test, that person will receive the crown of life that the Lord has promised to those who love *Him*! Hallelujah, I stand upon His promises that are yes and amen!

Psalm 116 became my favorite scripture!

I love the LORD because he hears my voice and my prayer for mercy. Because he bends down to listen, I will pray as long as I have breath! Death wrapped its ropes around me; the terrors of the grave overtook me. I saw only trouble and sorrow. Then I called on the name of the LORD: "Please, LORD, save me!" How kind the LORD is! How good he is! So merciful, this God of ours! The LORD protects those of childlike faith; I was facing death, and he saved me. Let my soul be at rest again, for the LORD has been good to me. He has saved me from death, my eyes from tears, my feet from stumbling. And so I walk in the LORD's presence as I live here on earth! I believed in You, so I said, "I am deeply troubled, LORD." In my anxiety I cried out to you, "These people are all liars!" What can I offer the LORD for all he has done for me? I will lift up the cup of salvation and praise the LORD's name for saving me. I will keep my promises to the LORD in the presence of all his people. The LORD cares deeply when His loved ones die. O LORD, I am your servant; yes, I am your servant, born into your household; you have freed me from my chains. I will offer you a sacrifice of thanksgiving and call on the name of the LORD. I will fulfill my vows to the LORD in the presence of all his people—in the house of the LORD in the heart of Jerusalem.

Praise the LORD!

I read this from one of my favorite morning devotionals "Streams in the Desert" on January 11. That made so much sense to me why sometimes we must suffer for Jesus Christ...

Comfort ye, comfort ye my people, saith your God. (Isaiah 40:1)

Store up comfort. This was the prophet's mission. The world is full of comfortless hearts, and ere thou art sufficient for this lofty ministry, thou must be Trained. And thy training is costly in the extreme; for, to render it perfect, thou too must pass through the same afflictions as are wringing countless hearts of tears and blood. Thus thy own life becomes the hospital ward where thou art taught the divine art of comfort. Thou art wounded, that in the binding up of thy wounds by the Great Physician, thou mayest learn how to render first aid to the wounded everywhere. Dost thou wonder why thou art passing through some special sorrow. Wait till ten years are passed, and thou wilt find many others afflicted as thou art. Thou wilt tell them how thou hast suffered and hast been comforted; then as the tale is unfolded, and the anodynes applied which once thy God wrapped around thee, in the eager look and the gleam of hope that shall chase the shadow of despair across the soul, thou shalt know why thou was afflicted, and bless God for the discipline that stored thy life with such A fund of experience and helpfulness.

God does not comfort us to make us comfortable, but to make us comforters. (Dr. Jowett in "Streams in the Desert," January 11)

More Testimonies of God's Faithfulness

- ### Len's God Moment with His Dad's Shotgun

Len went hunting today locally in Middleton, and as always I prayed for him to get his deer. When he came home though, he realized he left his rifle against a tree in the woods, and he began to panic because it was a loaded rifle. So I told him we needed to pray and give this to God and that no one would find the rifle, especially any young person walking through the woods. We called several police stations in the area to warn them that the rifle was loaded and abandoned in the woods and that Len would return to look for it the next morning. Len was not comfortable or happy about this since the rifle was his grandfather's, and he wanted to pass it on to his grandson one day. I knew God was in control, and this would end up being a wonderful testimony in the end. So the next morning, Len headed out to the woods, trying to remember the path he walked the prior day. Finally, I got a call that he found a note on one of the trees with a phone number in the area he remembered he had walked. The note said, "If you lost a rifle, call this number." He called the number, and Len went to meet the gentleman who was honest enough to find the rifle and leave a note to call him. Len was so grateful and thankful, and the two men became hunting buddies. I thank God for answering my prayers, for finding the rifle, for keeping it in safe hands, and for building up Len's faith on how very faithful God is and how He always answers prayer when you humbly ask Him.

- ### Supernatural Happening at My Chiropractor's Office

I had an appointment at my chiropractor's office today. However, my watch battery was not working, and since I did not realize that, I arrived one hour early to my appointment.

Now I needed to find a jeweler to go to after my appointment. So I mentioned it to the secretary that I needed to get a battery, so she advised me to go now since I was early, and she directed me to a jewelry store in a town in that area. When I got to the store, they did not have the tool necessary to fix my watch. So I went back to the doctor's office disappointed. Suddenly, an elderly lady entered the office quite bewildered and upset. She said that she had not been able to turn her car off because the key was stuck in the ignition. She said many neighbors tried but were unsuccessful. I asked her if I could try and she agreed. I asked her if I could pray first for God's wisdom and blessing and she agreed. She said she believed God knows everything that happens to her, and she believed that there are no accidents with God. She also said God has a reason why everything happens in life. I did share a couple of my supernatural miracles with her, and we praised God together. We went outside, and we laid hands on her car and simply asked God to help us and remove her keys from the ignition. Suddenly, the doctor came out, and we told him how we just prayed on her car because the key was stuck in the ignition. He stepped into her car, and the keys came right out! We were all praising God in the parking lot, and my quiet prayer was that God would soften the doctor's heart to believe in Jesus Christ, Who is the Son of God.

- The End of the Story… God's Miracle Working Power

After my appointment, I was driving to another jewelry store at the NSSC. I looked down on my wristwatch, and to my surprise, my watch was ticking, and it was the exact perfect time as on the clock on my car, with no new battery! "How could that be?" I asked myself. "Is God amazing or what"? My battery stopped working for others to witness the power of God and

His perfect timing so that He could bless an elderly woman and her chiropractor! Hallelujah! Praise God.

- Husband's Snoring Miracle

I have been married since May 3, 1996. One of my challenges was that he snored so bad even the neighbors could hear him on a warm summer night with the windows opened! It was so bad that I needed to take sleeping pills, wear earplugs, and pray every night for peace and for sanity and strength not to lose my mind! And believe me, there were nights of no sleep for weeks at a time, and those bad thoughts were as real as ever. No sleep even affected my heart. I thank God for the grace and strength to not commit a crime or get a divorce. This testimony happened about five years ago. Len even went to the hospital to a sleep disorder group and came home with a mask for sleep apnea that made him look like he was from outer space, and if you were in a deep sleep, that alone could drive you to fear and hysterics if you were awakened to that sight. However, that mask lasted about a week because Len suffered from claustrophobia, and he ripped it off within a week. So my snoring days continued day after day, week after week, month after month, and year after year until one night, God heard my cry! I was in my prayer room praying and crying out to my God, and I remember one of my favorite scriptures...

> God looks down from heaven on the
> entire human race; He looks to see if anyone is
> truly wise, if anyone seeks God. (Psalm 53:2)

Then God spoke so clearly to me as if HE was sitting right next to me! He said, "Why do you keep asking me to make him stop snoring when I have given you the power and authority that raised my Son Jesus from the dead and you can go into your bedroom and bind that devil of snoring who is trying to kill you, destroy your health with no sleep and frustration, and causing you to sin against your husband whom I love just as much as I love you? You are beginning to dislike him, and now you want to smother him with your pillow."

And believe me, I really was thinking of that many sleepless nights! I had even tried to push his body out of the bed with both my feet to get him to fall off the bed and stop snoring. If I would finally start to fall asleep, suddenly he would burst out, snoring which sounded like a locomotive train was crashing into my bedroom, causing me to wake up suddenly and fearfully. That was how loud his snoring was. Well, let me tell you, the power of God came on me like I was hit with a stroke of lightning! I picked up my Bible, as I was praying in the Holy Spirit, and I entered the bedroom with authority in Jesus's name. I placed my Bible on his chest, and I commanded that devil of snoring, disruption, anger, and frustration out of my bedroom and out of my husband. Suddenly he started choking, gurgling, and coughing, and I grabbed my Bible off of his chest and backed away slowly, out of shock! Within minutes, he fell back to sleep, only in a peaceful calm silence that was so quiet you could hear a pin drop. I softly and quietly left the room and went into my prayer room to praise and worship God and shouting for joy for the power of the Holy Spirit in me with thanksgiving and praise! I was actually doing my favorite victory dance as I praised God.

> Refrain from anger and turn from wrath;
> do not fret—it leads only to evil. (Psalm 37:8)

I humbly repented as I cried out to Him for help in Psalm 77:1–7,

> I cried out to God for help; I cried out
> to God to hear me. When I was in distress, I

sought the Lord; at night I stretched out untiring hands, and I would not be comforted. I remembered you, God, and I groaned; I meditated, and my spirit grew faint. You kept my eyes from closing; I was too troubled to speak. I thought about the former days, the years of long ago; I remembered my songs in the night. My heart meditated and my spirit asked: "Will the Lord reject forever? Will he never show his favor again?" (Psalm 77:1–7)

I prayed to the LORD, and he answered me. He freed me from all my fears. Those who look to him for help will be radiant with joy; no shadow of shame will darken their faces. In my desperation I prayed, and the LORD listened; he saved me from all my troubles. (Psalm 34:4–6)

I then read Psalm 34:4–17, and I was so blessed I could hardly contain my joy.

I sought the LORD, and he answered me; he delivered me from all my fears. Those who look to him are radiant; their faces are never covered with shame. This poor man [woman] called, and the LORD heard him [her]; he saved him [her] out of all his [her] troubles. The angel of the LORD encamps around those who fear Him, and he delivers them. Taste and see that the LORD is good; blessed is the one who takes refuge in Him. Fear the LORD, you His holy people, for those who fear Him lack nothing. Come, my children, listen to me; I will teach you the fear of the LORD. Whoever of you loves life and desires to see many good days, keep your tongue from evil and your lips from telling lies. Turn from evil and do good; seek peace and pursue it. The eyes of the LORD are on the righteous, and His ears are attentive to their cry. The righteous cry out, and the LORD hears them; He delivers them from all their troubles.

He has never snored since, and that was about five years now. And that was one of my most favorite testimonies from my awesome, faithful, and powerful God. So now, years later, my husband tells me I am snoring and I say, "Then pray over me and command that demon of snoring to leave my body in Jesus's precious name." But he said my snoring doesn't bother him. I just hate to think that I really snore!

• Len's Hunting Story and Miracle

Len was going hunting today locally, and I asked him to pray with me before he left the house. We asked God to bless him with a deer because in the past, he never wanted me to pray with him, but this day, God instructed me to ask him to pray, and he did. Matthew 18:20 said,

When two or more agree on anything in prayer He is in our midst.

And I said, "We must humble ourselves before God and just admit for once that you need him at all times, even to find a deer."

When he got home, he said he not only saw four deer coming right to him, but he was able to get one with his bow and arrow. But the deer did not die. That saddened Len so much that he did not have the heart to leave him there to die, but he could not even find him. He tracked the blood but still no deer. He couldn't even sleep that night worrying about the deer. So the next morning, he called his friends Dave and Rob to come over and help him locate the deer and take it out of its misery. They found the deer, thank God, and he called the police because it was Sunday, and you could not kill or hunt on Sunday. God so graciously had the police kill the deer, and they were able to take it and have it gutted for venison meat. God is so good and so faithful when we pray and ask God for help, guidance, and whatever else we need of HIM.

> Rejoice always, pray without ceasing, and give thanks in all circumstances, for this is the will of God in Christ Jesus for you. (1 Thessalonians 5:16–17)

- A Testimony at the Swimming Pool

I had another God moment today while we were living in sunny Florida. We decided to go to the pool for a swim and cool off as it was very hot that day. There were only three other people in the pool, so we were floating around on our floats. Then one woman who was on her noodle at the opposite end of the pool started to approach us.

She then said, "Hi, can I ask you a question?" as she was pointing to Lenny.

He said, "Sure, can I help you?"

She said, "Do you ride your bike every morning around 9:00 a.m.?"

He said yes, and she said, "I knew I recognized you, because you have such great posture while you ride, and you ride a woman's bike, and I recognize your baseball cap." She said, "I have my coffee every morning on my lanai, and I watch you go by every day."

Well, we all laughed, and then Len asked her where she lived, and she explained the house, color, and location. Then something clicked in my head…the yellow house next to the golf club. I then said, "I know of you."

Her eyes widened as she floated closer to me now and asked, "How did you know?"

So I began to explain how I knew who she was in the yellow house. My story went like this…

About two and a half years ago, I was trying to rent a home in this community, and I kept calling a realtor I came to know. But she quickly told me she did not do rentals so she couldn't help me. But every time I prayed, the Lord told me to call her again. So every week I called her and asked if she knew of a rental at the park. She kept reminding me that she could not help me. But God kept telling me in prayer to persist calling her, so I did. Every week I gave her a call. I was so determined to rent a house there to visit my best friend who lived there. She was diagnosed with a rare form of Alzheimer's disease, and I needed to get there to visit her soon. Therefore, she and I kept praying that a house would be available for me and my husband to rent for a month so we could all be together. Meanwhile, my husband was not fond of Florida and really did not want to go. But my friend and I persisted in prayer for a house and begging my husband to come with me so I could pray and be with others who needed prayer at the park. So this all happened in January through March, and one Saturday night in March, my phone rang.

When I answered, a woman said, "Hi, I am the realtor you keep calling me for a rental home in Florida. Are you the woman who keeps calling me every week?"

I responded, "Yes, it's me, do you have some good news for me?"

She laughed as I told her my dilemma and why I kept calling her and how I wanted to visit my best friend who was ill. Well, funny thing is, she said, "I know your friend very well, and we attend the same church." Then she said, "I think God answered your prayers because I am visiting friends here in Florida and they need to get back to Canada, and they asked me if I knew anyone who wanted to sublease their house for a month beginning April 1. Then I remembered you, and I am so glad you gave me your phone number."

So we were all so excited and immediately made the necessary arrangements to fly to Florida. They were told that I was a prayer warrior and an intercessor, so they told me about their best friend who lived in the park and asked me if I would pray for her as well. They told me that she just lost her husband and that one of her daughters died of cancer. Then shortly thereafter, she too was diagnosed with cancer and was very ill in the hospital. They asked if I would please pray for their friend who lived in the yellow house on the corner. I told her I would pray for her every day from that point on. So that is the history of the gal on the float in the pool.

As I was telling her the story in the pool, I told her I had never stopped praying for her and I often wanted to knock on her door to see how she was doing, but the car was not the same as it was back then. Therefore, I was apprehensive to knock on the door. I prayed that she would still be alive, but I had no way of knowing, so I just kept praying. Then she said that she got a different car. By now we were sharing, and we were so connected, and she asked me if she could just touch me. We then embraced, both shedding our tears of love and praise to God, and then I prayed over her. She said she was heading back to her hometown but that she would never forget me. She said she too became a prayer warrior since her diagnosis and that she was on a few prayer chains as well. We both shared our miracle of healing in Jesus's name. That was a very special "God moment." I am praising God for always answering prayer on His timing and in His way. Hallelujah, and praise God forevermore. It is amazing how many women God has put in my path for friendship, prayer, healing, and salvation! I have given up the count!

> So you see, the Lord knows how to rescue
> godly people from their trials. (2 Peter 2:9a)

- Another Answered Prayer

I was on the golf course in Florida today when I got a call from my daughter, and she was pretty upset. Her son was playing baseball, and another kid stole his wallet out of his gym bag. It had his charge cards, driver's license, and other important information. Now she had to make several calls to issue new charge cards and license. I prayed with her that whoever took the wallet, God would convict him to have the heart to return it to him immediately. Within hours, the boy found his telephone number, and he was convicted to return the wallet, and nothing was taken. We all praised God for His faithfulness and the power of prayer.

- My New Friend Gives Her Life to Jesus

I was introduced to a woman today at the golf course that was willing to play golf with me. I was so excited when she and her friend invited me to join them. I was drawn to her because she reminded me of my deceased mother and dear friend, whom I missed and loved. We immediately hit it off and began playing golf together. While we hung out together, I shared many testimonies of how God has blessed me over the years and also shared my testimony of salvation. One day after church, I put a card from the church under the door, inviting her to visit. When I asked her if she got the card on her back door, she replied yes, and also got two of them. I laughed and told her she had better come to church since God sent her two invitations, and she agreed. She accepted the invitation and we took her to church the following Sunday. The miracle gets better because when I went home for the summer, she not only continued to attend church services, but she took my best friend too. She picked her up at the Memory Cottage every Sunday. They went to Bible study classes and then out to breakfast. She continues to befriend Donna, attends church, and takes her to the pool and visits her at Parkside Memory Cottage where she lives. I am so blessed to hear of this great miracle.

Angie and I spoke today, and she told me she was praying to God that she might hear from her daughter, who has been estranged from her for a few years. And just as she was about to call her, the phone rang, and she called her and she was so blessed to reconnect with her daughters and share the love of God with them. Angie's other daughter spent the summer with her in Florida and she is blessed to see God rekindle her daughters' love and friendship. I am thankful that God has touched their hearts. She has since shared many miracles of how God has blessed her and her family and we praise God for His faithfulness and love! We attend Bible study, we fellowship at the same church, and we are great golf buddies as well!

• My Computer Crashes Now That I Am about Finished with My Book!

I was typing my book, and I had just about completed my story when the computer screen turned black! *Horrified* does not come close to how I was feeling that night. I had been trying to complete this book since God has told me to write it. A few years ago, when I started this book, my computer crashed, and I lost the all my notes and hard work. I was then so devastated that I never started writing it again. God kept telling me to write the book in many of my journal entries over the years, but I just did not want to. Sometimes I even felt rebellious for not obeying God. I was just so frustrated when I lost all my notes and thought God didn't care. So here I am in that same position and crying out to God frustrated and disappointed. So I called Comcast to come over the next day, Saturday, because I noticed that the cable cord was hanging out of the wall. I thought that was the reason my computer just stopped working. Then again, I always blamed the devil who does not want me to write my book and glorify God, or perhaps God allowed these hindrances to happen in my life to see if I really trusted Him.

That night I cried out to my God and said to Him, "If this is Your book and You told me to write it, then can You fix my computer? If not, then I've believed a lie, and I let it all go and nail it to Your cross. I ask only that Your will be done, Lord."

I felt a peace in me that transcends all understanding. I just went to bed and slept like a baby. Then at 8:30 a.m., I was awakened by Comcast at my door. A woman came in and went to my computer, and I told her I was writing a book and I needed to know if it could be saved. It was fixed in no time, and then she asked what my book was about. I hesitated, won-

dering if I should even share this with her, and I secretly prayed
and asked God's permission. I felt His peace in my heart, and I
told her the book was about my life of abuse, drugs, and alcohol and how God delivered me and told me to write this book.
She told me she wanted to write a book too because she too
was a victim of child abuse, rape, drugs, and alcohol. She then
shared her story with me that she and her partner were both
abused and raped as children and have had to deal with drugs
and alcohol addictions. We shared our story together, and we
were convinced that this was not a mistake that she took my call
but that God wanted us to meet. She asked me for a copy of
my book when it is published, and I promised her that I would
pray for her and her partner to accept Jesus Christ Who can set
them free. There are no accidents with God. He allows these
things to happen to me for a reason, and that reason is to set
other captives free.

> Commit your way to the LORD, trust
> also in Him, and He will do it. (Psalm 37:5)

The Power of Prayer

Isn't that the same for Christians who are afflicted, storm-
tossed, and without comfort? Until the storms and difficulties
allowed by God's providence beat upon a believer again and
again, his character appears flawed and blurred. Yet the trials
actually clear away the clouds and shadows, perfect the form of
His character, and bestow brightness and blessings to our life!

Therefore, our prayers are God's opportunities. So can I
ask you if you are sorrowful? Then pray to our faithful God
Who can make your affliction sweet and give you strength. Are
you in gladness? Prayer can add to your joy with a sweet-sa-
voring perfume. Are you in extreme danger from outward or
inward enemies? Prayer can set at your right hand an angel of

God whose touch could shatter a millstone and who will obey the voice of His Word as you speak it boldly with belief that God will perform it in your life. Be victorious in Him! But prayer is the link that connects us with God. This is the bridge that spans every gulf and bears us over every abyss of danger or of need. God said in 1 Thessalonians 5:17,

Never stop praying!

And I believe Him. I have realized that tragedy, trials, and tribulations can either destroy us or make us stronger. I choose to become stronger in Him who lives in Me.

Do we know the power of our supernatural weapon? Do we dare to use it with the authority of a faith that commands as well as asks? My prayer is that God will baptize us with holy audacity and divine confidence! He does not want great men, but He wants men and women who will dare to prove the *greatness* of their *God.*

But while Peter was in prison, the church prayed very earnestly for him. (Acts 12:5)

And he was set free! It reminds me of that day in 1979 when the prayer warriors interceded for me when I was about to commit suicide.

God said, the prayers of the righteous are powerful and effective. Hallelujah! (James 5:16)

My suffering was good for me for it taught me to pay attention to God's decrees. (Psalm 119:71)

You keep track of all my sorrows. You have collected all my tears in your bottle. You have recorded each one in your book. For you have *rescued* me from death; you have kept my feet from slipping.

So now I can walk in your presence, O God, in your life-giving light. (Psalm 56:8-13)

I write this book not to prove that God answers all my prayers, but yes He does in His perfect timing and He is always faithful. I share my story to provide evidence that I am a living monument of God's Amazing Grace. I will praise and honor my God forevermore.

Ephesians 2:4-10 New Living Translation (NLT)

But God is so rich in mercy, and he loved us so much, that even though we were dead because of our sins, he gave us life when he raised Christ from the dead. (It is only by God's grace that you have been saved!) For he raised us from the dead along with Christ and seated us with him in the heavenly realms because we are united with Christ Jesus. So God can point to us in all future ages as examples of the incredible wealth of his grace and kindness toward us, as shown in all he has done for us who are united with Christ Jesus.

God saved you by his grace when you believed. And you can't take credit for this; it is a gift from God. Salvation is not a reward for the good things we have done, so none of us can boast about it. For we are God's masterpiece. He has created us anew in Christ Jesus, so we can do the good things he planned for us long ago.

I continue to press toward the goal to see Jesus. I don't mean to say that I have already achieved these things or that I have already reached perfection. But I press on to possess that perfection for which Christ Jesus first possessed me. No, dear brothers and sisters, I have not achieved it, but I focus on this one thing: Forgetting the past and looking forward to what lies ahead, I press on to reach the end of the race and receive the heavenly prize for which God, through Christ Jesus, is calling us. Hallelujah and Amen! (Philippians 3:12-14)

Now, as I conclude this book, I would like to share some funny God moments with my first grandchild, William, who has brought so much love, joy, and encouragement to my life during the years of trials and tribulations. His love for me filled my heart with courage to never give up. He was the gift from God that brought me so much joy when I thought my time on earth was done.

- Here Are a Few "Funny God Moments" with My Grandson Will

1. Will insisted on getting a cowboy hat so he could ride his play horse we got him for Christmas. He said to me, "Why didn't you think of that when you got me the horse, Grammy?"

   "Hmmm" I thought, "why didn't I?"

   So we went shopping that day for a cowboy hat. We could not find one in any of the department stores or even Toys R Us. So we sat in my car and prayed and asked God where we could find his cowboy hat. The idea instantly came to me, and I said, "Let's look in the party store in the strip mall in Peabody."

   I recall just looking up and down the aisles and was getting frustrated. Then Will ran to the man stocking the shelves and said, "Excuse me, can you tell me where my cowboy hat is?"

"Hmmm," the man said, "I don't think we carry them."

Will confidently answered, "Oh yes, it is here because we prayed in Grammy's car, and God said it was in here."

The man chuckled and said, "Then let's go find the hat."

Cowboy hat

Sure enough, he went out back and came out with Will's cowboy hat. We all were so excited, and we kept thanking God as we did our victory dance. The man was so happy to bless Will too.

Playing policeman—office

2. I babysat for Will every Monday and Tuesday, so we played make-believe imaginary games like school days, hospital days, policeman, fire house, etc. Will asked me for a medical kit so we could play hospital that day. So he explained to me that God told him the medical kit was at the Hallmark Store. "I doubt that, Will, I think they only have cards there." He insisted God told him, so I drove there, and sure enough, there was his medical kit, and it was the last one on the shelf. The faith of the little child won my heart again.

3. Another great God moment was at a sleepover at Will's house, and he was only two years old. While I was tucking Will into bed and we were about to do our prayers, he asked me to pray over a cut he had on his eye. "Of course," I said, and I continued to pray. He then asked me to sleep with him for a bit until he fell asleep, and I willingly lay down next to him. Within minutes, he sat up and said, God told me to pray for you, Grammy. I had told him that day while we were playing outdoors that my feet hurt. I answered him and said, "Sure," so I sat up and handed him my foot. He held my foot up to God and asked Him to heal my foot so I could keep visiting him and play with him forever. Then he said, "Holy Mary, mother of God…" And he finished the prayer to Mary. God used the faith of a small child to manifest my healing, and my feet were perfect after that.

4. Another great "God moment" at Will's house was when we walked every day, on very adventurous trips, singing songs and praising God. He loved squirrels, so we followed them around the town. We had lunch at Friendly's because Will loved their hot dogs and their free vanilla ice cones for dessert. We stopped at the

toy store and played with the trains because Thomas the Train was one of his most favorite pastimes. We played with the trains just about every day that we spent together.

He loved Thomas the Train

One day we were singing "This Is the Day That the Lord Has Made" and keeping up the beat of the song as we walked and sang. The funny story is that on the following Sunday, when we were at a Solemn High Mass at the Catholic Church with his family, the choir began to sing that same song... "This Is the Day That the Lord Has Made"...only in a slow, drawn-out beat that sounded so depressing to me, but I just sat and said nothing. Finally, Will at age three, stood up on the pew and said, "Excuse me, sir, you are not singing that song right, it's too slow," as he became adamant and singing it with the beat I had taught him from the Pentecostal Church! Of course, people around us, including his parents, got embarrassed, but I chuckled and took him outside to tell them they just sang it in a different way. That was a very precious memory for sure.

5. Will was becoming my best prayer partner now. One Thanksgiving Day, after having dinner at Uncle

Ronnie's house, we were headed to our aunt's house in Newton for dessert. We had to stop and pull over because an ambulance was coming. Will immediately commented, "Grammy, we need to pray for someone in the ambulance for God to heal them." We prayed, and then Will said that he prayed for people at night when God told him to, like people in New York and Florida and all over the world. He was so precious! He could become an intercessor like his Grammy!

6. This is one of my favorite times while lying down with Will, as I did all the time before I left his house to go home. I really was tired and actually falling asleep, but Will kept asking me questions. Finally, I told him I needed to nap before driving home, so I said good night and kissed him again. Suddenly, I peeked and saw him looking up to the heavens, and he began to pray to God the following prayer... "Dear God, I just love my Grammy so much. I was wondering if you could lock all the doors in my house so Grammy cannot go home so she can live with me. Hmmm, if you cannot do that, how about making her so small and hiding her in one of my story books so I can see her every day when I read my books? Well, that's my prayer, God, and I thank you."

    Then he was throwing kisses to God in heaven. I had to hide under the sheet because I was crying so much. How I love this child. Father God I thank you for this special gift!

Will saying bye to Grammy

7. When Will's computer game would not work, Will told his mommy to just stop and pray like Grammy does and the game will work. So Amy prayed with Will, and the computer game worked, and Amy called to tell me, and they were so happy! She was actually crying with amazement as I was!

8. Then Will and Mommy prayed for a new car, but she only had $19,000; she could not find a car for that money. Will prayed again, and the Toyota salesman gave her the car for that exact amount of money that they prayed for. Will and Amy were so happy, praising God.

9. The family was going to have a surprise sixtieth birthday party for me, but it was forecast to rain all weekend. Will prayed and asked God to give me a perfect sunny day, and God heard his prayer, and the day was such a beautiful sunny day. It rained on Sunday, so Will told his parents they needed to go to church to thank God for giving Grammy a sunny day for her birthday party!

10. At Will's graduation from nursery school in 2006, the teacher asked him what his favorite time was at Holy

Name School. Will answered, "Learning about my God and His love!"

My grandson is now a sophomore at Boston College, the college of his dreams and our answered prayers. I will forever thank God for my first grandson who gave me hope and a will to live and not die.

Will goes to BC

I have been so richly blessed with the lives of my four children and eight grandchildren. Their love, joy and laughter have helped me during my journey to healing and wholeness and I am forever grateful to God for all of them, and for His amazing grace and love.

Great is the Lord! He is most worthy of praise! No one can measure His greatness. Let each generation tell its children of Your mighty acts; let them proclaim Your power and I will proclaim Your greatness forevermore! (Psalm 145:3-4)

Blessed with two children and 4 grandkids and 2 step-daughters and 4 step-grandkids God is soooo good.

This is my son and his family

This is my daughter and her family

Deceased stepdaughter and her sons

This is stepdaughter and her family

A Word from the Author

As a prayer warrior in the army of the Living God, I have faced many trials and challenges to overcome in all the years of my life. But through it all I have learned to trust in Jesus and to overcome by the Blood of the Lamb and the word of my testimony. I have made the sovereign Lord my shelter, and I will always tell everyone about the wonderful things He has done for me and through me. Hallelujah forevermore!

After reading my story, I ask if you believe in miracles? Do you know what a miracle is? According to *Webster's Dictionary* it is...

1. A surprising and welcome event that is not explicable by natural or scientific laws and is therefore considered to be the work of a divine agency.
2. A highly improbable or extraordinary event, development, or accomplishment that brings very welcome consequences.
3. An amazing product or achievement, or an outstanding example of something.

A biblical definition is very similar...

> An effect or extraordinary event in the physical world that surpasses all known human or natural powers and is ascribed to a supernatural cause.
> Such an effect or event manifesting or considered as a work of God.
> A wonder, a marvel.

Hallelujah!

I choose to praise the Living God, the Almighty God Who created heaven and earth, and I will tell the world of His marvelous deeds forevermore!

Shout joyful praises to God, all the earth. Sing about the glory of His Name! Tell the world how glorious He is. Say to God, "How awesome are Your deeds!" Amen! (Psalm 66)

God has commanded me to give thanks to my Lord and to proclaim His greatness to all. Let the whole world know all He has done for me. So I come to glorify His name...because He has known me before the foundations of this world. He had a perfect plan for my life, and Satan has been trying to kill and destroy that plan for my life all of my days. I have told you the story of my wonderful Counselor, the Anchor of my soul, the Captain of my salvation, my Consuming Fire, my Deliverer, my God of all comfort and peace, my God of all hope, my God of all grace, my God of all love, because He is Love. And that is what I promised Him I would do. I would rejoice and tell the world how awesome He is and has been all my life. And I will rejoice always and worship only Him and no other gods. He is my Redeemer, my Sanctifier, and the Shepherd of my soul. And He is strong and mighty in battle. He is my Helper, my High Tower, my everlasting Hope, my Rock of Refuge, my Shield, my Salvation, my Song, my Support, my Refiner and Purifier, my Refuge from the storms, the Strength of my life, the Reward to those who seek Him, my Stronghold, my Sun and Shield, my Sure Foundation, my True Light, my Eternal Life, the Way, the Truth, and the Life, the Bread of Heaven, my Living Water, my Wisdom, my Counselor, the Word of God, the Word of Life, my Confidence, my Lamb of God Who takes away the sins of the world, my Shade, my King of Kings, my Maker and the Lover of my Soul, my Husband, my Brother, my Father, my All-in-All.

I cannot and will not live without Him. I will continue to search for Him and His strength and continue to seek Him all the days of my life. I will remember the wonderful deeds He has performed and the many miracles He has done through His servant and His chosen ones. Yes, He is the Lord my God, and His justice is seen throughout all the land. He always stands by His covenant and the commitment He made to a thousand generations. Yes, His covenant is a never-ending covenant to all His people! He asks one thing of us, and that is to only *believe*. Yes, Lord, I believe, yes, I believe. Because no fire can burn me, no battle can turn me away from you, no mountain can stop me from proclaiming you, and no giant can defeat me because You know me, You know my name, and I know You talk to me and You tell me I am Your beloved. You own me and hold me with your righteous right hand, and You will never leave me or forsake me. Oh, how You comfort me, counsel me, and tell me I am Your friend. Yes, You know my name because You formed me in my mother's womb, and You named me then before I was even born.

I believe that I was named by my Lord Jesus before the foundations of this world! "Before I formed you in the womb I knew you, before you were born I set you apart." (Jeremiah 1:5a)

"Carol Ann Drinkwater" which means as follows:

Carol: Song of Joy—How I love to sing His songs of Joy.
Ann: Grace of God—He has blessed me with His Grace.
Drinkwater: I am drinking His living water.
Hallelujah!!!

"I will drink the Living Water all the days of my life, and I will eat Your bread of life! Amen."

Now all glory to God Who is able, through his mighty power at work within us, to accomplish infinitely more than we might ask or think. Glory to Him in the church and in Christ Jesus through all generations forever and ever! Amen.

YOUR LIFE IS YOUR LEGACY, SO MAKE IT A GOOD ONE!

> In that day you will sing: "I will praise you, O LORD! You were angry with me, but not anymore. Now You comfort me. See, God has come to save me. I will trust in Him and not be afraid. The LORD GOD is my strength and my song; He has given me victory." (Isaiah 12)
>
> With joy you will drink deeply from the fountain of salvation! In that wonderful day you will sing: "Thank the LORD! Praise His name! Tell the nations what He has done. Let them know how mighty He is! Sing to the LORD, for He has done wonderful things. Make known His praise around the world. Let all the people of Jerusalem shout His praise with joy! For great is the Holy One of Israel who lives among you." (Isaiah 50:4)

We must be the LORD's obedient servants…

The Sovereign LORD has given me His words of wisdom so that I know how to comfort the weary. Morning by morning He awakens me and opens my understanding to do His will. I am *Forever Rescued* and a child of God; therefore, I am no longer a slave to fear! I sing Hallelujah and praise God forevermore.

It will never be THE END!

Epilogue

Testimony in Memory of My Stepdaughter Nicole
(1971–2019)

How many parents in this world whose hopes and dreams have been shattered by rebellious, hurting children? That is how life was with my stepdaughter Nicole. She resented me for marrying her father over twenty-three years ago. For many years I have witnessed her coming to the end of her journey in life from her family and faith in God. I watched her loved ones suffer as she would overdose on drugs and alcohol and then be hospitalized for weeks at a time. She suffered from liver failure, along with diabetes, chronic pancreatitis, lung issues, herpes, and thrush. She would be bedridden and then given days to live and in hospice care several times. She would then recover, come back to life, and hospice would leave. I always believed that God's grace was giving her another chance to live. We had prayed for her, we prayed over her, and finally she got baptized in water at her sister's church. The sad news was that after her baptism, she did not get healed as she had hoped. She became angry and disappointed with God. We were unable to neither talk about Jesus nor pray for her. She estranged herself from us all except for her dad, who was always there for her when she needed him. However, her family never stopped praying for her and believing God that He would bring His prodigal daughter home.

When our loved ones wander from the heart of God, the most powerful thing to do is pray. Being intercessors, her sister and I never gave up praying and interceding for Nicole.

When I heard about the book *Promises for Prodigals* by Lori Wilkerson Stewart, I ordered it immediately. She mentioned in her book that you may not save them, but you can declare God's promises over them, and that is what I did. In fact, while in Florida this winter, God gave me instructions for Nicole. He told me to be in prayer every evening when my husband went to bed and to be still and trust God who would instruct me to write Nicole a letter but sign it from Jesus Christ her Lord. I agreed in faith to obey God and to read a chapter in the book every evening and then to sit quietly in His presence and pray for Nicole, meditating on His Word. I would pray in the Holy Spirit and wait on God for a promise for Nicole.

I remember one night I became fearful that if I mailed the letters, perhaps Nicole would resent me even more. I then asked God what to do if that happened. He said fear not because the letters were not from me but from her God who loved her more than she could ever know. He said my job was to be "His Ready Writer" and to obey Him and He would tell me what to write and when to mail them. I obeyed God faithfully, and there were days that I had two or three letters on my desk waiting for God to tell me when to mail one. Some nights I would just cry for hours because the letters were so anointed and abounding with

His love for her that I could hardly contain my emotions. In the past, I told God how difficult it was for me to like Nicole because the rejection was just too painful, but He said He would love her through me if I would just be an empty vessel to be used by Him. As I faithfully obeyed God, I was amazed at how my heart was full of His forgiveness, compassion, and never-ending love for her.

About six months had passed and we returned to our summer home in Massachusetts. One day as I was parking my car to go into Wal-Mart, my cell phone rang. To my surprise it was Nicole. I was shocked because she never called me; she only called her dad. When I answered, she was crying and thanking me for the letters I had been writing to her. She then asked me how I knew what she was suffering from. I told her that I did not know, but that God did and He told me to write those letters and sign them from Him not me. She kept crying in unbelief, and she said every letter came precisely on the day she was suffering and it was exactly what she needed to hear. She kept thanking me, asking me to forgive her, and telling me how sorry she was for rejecting me all those years. I told her I forgave her long ago and that Jesus in me loved her more than she could ever imagine. I then began to minister the love of Christ to her, praying for her, and leading her closer to the love of Jesus. By the end of this telephone conversation, we both were crying, praising God for His forgiveness and love.

She called again a few days later saying she felt so good that she was able to finally get out of bed. She said she and her fiancé went out shopping and enjoyed that day for the first time in months. I kept praising God and giving Him all the glory and honor due Him.

This is the end of her story though…

Nicole was hospitalized two weeks before Christmas when her doctors told her that there was nothing more they can do for her because her life was about to end and she must be prepared to meet her Maker. Her dad, sister, and I were in the room when the doctors gave her this devastating news; she had to make a choice whether to go home and die or go to a hospice facility. She was now willing for her dad, her sister, and I to pray for her to accept Jesus Christ and His perfect will for her life. We all cried as God filled us with His peace and love. She decided to be transferred to a beautiful hospice facility where she was able to receive the compassionate comfort care she needed as she faced this fearful terminal illness. Hospice provided her the relief from the painful symptoms and the physical and mental stress of this life-limiting illness that was now taking her life. We were all blessed and comforted during this heartbreaking process. We could not have endured without the love from our Lord Jesus Christ.

Her family, her sons, and her former husband spent the last week of her life at her bedside as God poured out His love, His forgiveness, and His peace over all of us. It was a week of healing and deliverance as God sutured the wounds of our broken hearts and filled us with His amazing love and grace. Jesus escorted Nicole to her heavenly home on Christmas evening 2019. Although we all miss Nicole, we are blessed that she is finally healed, set free, and at peace. We believe that Nicole is in heaven resting in the arms of her loving Lord and Savior Jesus Christ.

I am blessed and thankful that I obeyed God and for the great faith to believe that He would save His daughter. His promises are guaranteed because each promise of God is honored by His mighty Name (Psalm 138:2). God is forever faithful and His Word is so alive and active, sharper than any two-edged sword, pulling down the strongholds of the enemy (Hebrews 4:12)! I will continue to fight the good fight of faith for those God tells me to pray for until my work here on earth is complete and one day, I too will join my loved ones in heaven for all eternity. Hallelujah forevermore!

About the Author

Carol was born and raised in Massachusetts and began her education at Tufts University in Boston as a certified dental assistant and worked in that field for several years. When she married and had children, she then continued her education in early childhood to teach kindergarten, as she always wanted to be the first teacher in a child's life. After completing courses in early childhood education at Salem State University in Salem and Wheelock College in Boston, Carol wrote a grant and received the necessary funding to implement the first family day care center in the Middlesex County of Massachusetts.

When her children grew older, she pursued and acquired a challenging career as a legal assistant and worked in many law firms in Boston and the North Shore. Her last employment before retirement was with the North Shore Elder Services as an Administrative Assistant supporting the elderly in the Money Management Department.

When Carol accepted Jesus Christ as her Lord and Savior in 1979, she set different goals to achieve God's plan for her life. She then felt called to serve as God's ambassador as she became involved in her local Pentecostal church. God gave her the great commission for souls becoming an intercessor with deep faith, undying love, constant hope, tenacious conviction, and a profound insight inspired by God. She stood courageously for the truth in God's holy Word, knowing Him personally and being empowered by His Holy Spirit. She has become a great warrior in the Lord's army praying daily for the world and bringing His light both individually and corporately. Because God has blessed Carol with love and compassion for the elderly, she began a nursing home ministry at her church, transforming broken lives and bringing new life in obedience to God Who has worked powerfully through her. She trained volunteers to visit nursing homes in her area, bringing the Good News to the shut-ins in hospitals and nursing facilities with a passion for Jesus Christ as she still ministers to this day. God has continued to be her companion, her captain, her victory, her resource, her divine energy, and her anointing as He sends her out to do His work with the assurance that all tasks He assigns for her is achieved through His Holy Spirit. Carol is honored to be included in God's redemptive plan for the world. This is Carol's first book, and she is thankful and grateful to Him for calling her to be His pen of a ready writer.

She is the mother of two children and two stepchildren and has eight grandchildren to whom she devotes her love and time when able. Carol has since retired to live in Florida during the winter months where she enjoys blessing God's children and bicycling and golf in her free time.

CPSIA information can be obtained
at www.ICGtesting.com
Printed in the USA
LVHW050349130721
692461LV00001B/70